Smart Retirement

Critical Things You Should Know Before Cashing Your Last Paycheck

Thomas S. Stephens

(713) 416-0157

tom@tsswealth.com

Securities offered through Cambridge Investment Research, Inc. A Registered Broker/Dealer (Member FINRA/SIPC)
Advisory services offered through Cambridge Investment Research Advisors, Inc. A Registered Investment Advisor

Copyright © 2019 by Thomas S. Stephens
All rights reserved. No Part of this book may be reproduced, scanned, or distributed in any printed or electronic form without permission.
Third Edition: July, 2020
Printed in the United States of America
ISBN: 9781794563575
07172020

Smart Retirement

Other Books by Thomas S. Stephens

The Cost of Aging:
Finding Resources to Meet the Financial Demands of Aging

Planning for Tomorrow:
Essential Guide to Having Your Affairs in Order

Our Aging Parents:
Comprehensive Guide to Caring for Aging Loved Ones

Survivor's Handbook:
Essential Guide to Financial Matters after a Death

Find these books on amazon.com

Smart Retirement

Dedication

This book is dedicated to my late wife, Louella A. Peca, and to all those who have fought the good fight but are no longer with us.

Disclaimer

The information provided in this text is general in nature, does not take into consideration the reader's personal circumstances, and is therefore not intended to be a substitute for specific, individualized financial, legal, and tax advice. For advice specific to your own personal circumstances, we suggest that you consult with qualified and properly licensed financial, legal, and/or tax professionals.

Tax laws and provisions are subject to change. The author, Cambridge Investment Research, Inc. and Cambridge Investment Research Advisors, Inc. do not offer tax or legal advice or services. All entities and programs mentioned in this book are not affiliated with nor endorsed by the author, Cambridge Investment Research, Inc. or Cambridge Investment Research Advisors, Inc.

There is no assurance that the techniques and strategies mentioned are suitable for all individuals or will yield positive outcomes.

Finally, references to various websites, products, and companies are not an endorsement, but are merely provided as general information purposes.

Smart Retirement

Table of Contents

Introduction vii

Chapter 1: Retire With Purpose 1

Chapter 2: The Money Question? 7

Chapter 3: Retirement Plans & Investment Accounts.... 13

Chapter 4: Lifetime Income Strategies 21

Chapter 5: Tax Free Retirement Income 27

Chapter 6: Social Security 13

Chapter 7: Healthcare Costs in Retirement................ 41

Chapter 8: Understanding Medicare 45

Chapter 9: Understanding Medicaid 51

Chapter 10: Long Term Care 53

Chapter 11: Advance Directives 65

Chapter 12: Wills and Estates 77

Chapter 13: Hiring Professional Advisors 85

Appendix Section .... Appendix

Smart Retirement

Introduction

About the Author

My name is **Tom Stephens** and I bring a unique perspective to Retirement Planning, Wealth Management, and the topics in this book: first, as Cryptographer in the US Air Force during the Vietnam War, I gained the Perspective of Military Discipline, Being a Team Player, and Looking Out for My Brothers. Next, as a Senior Executive in a large Commercial Bank, I gained an understanding of how money is managed; third, the perspective of leaving the safety of a large corporate environment to create a successful consulting firm, gaining an understanding of all aspects of running a small business. Finally, or so I thought, I gained the perspective of a financially comfortable retirement, based on sound planning and investment strategies with incomes for life; but then, tragically, the perspective of being a caregiver and widower, gaining an understanding of the human side of catastrophic illness, along with all its Financial Implications; that in turn, led to becoming an author and speaker, publishing workbooks and presenting workshops to assist others in planning for Retirement and other major life events.

In summary, then, this book was written from a very unique perspective, in that it is virtually all based on my personal life experiences, a path that I walked, and not based on theories researched or hypothesized: I have been retired, living on a fixed income, and know the apprehension of watching a volatile stock market; I turned on Social Security early for very specific, thought-out reasons; I enrolled in Medicare and now understand the advantages and disadvantages of all the various options; I had to place my father in Assisted Living due to end-stage Parkinson's disease, I gained a thorough understanding of Long Term Care; and finally, I was there with my wife through 13 months of chemotherapy and then in Hospice when she breathed her last breath.

I have now returned to work as an Investment Advisor, focused on helping my clients create and monitor successful Retirement strategies, following and using Conservative Investment approaches that have worked and are working in my life.

In summary, then, I want to say that life is a collage of successes, failures, happiness, and sometimes sadness, but regardless of what life offers, having a Retirement Plan in place and having your finances under control can bring an enormous peace of mind during the last third of your life. I sincerely hope that this book is a great benefit to you, and I am personally available to become your valued Advisor.

Tom Stephens
Houston, Texas

About the Text
This text was originally written to accompany a live seminar of the same name, although the information is formatted and presented in such a way that it can be read and used as a stand-alone reference manual. In either event, the goal was to both inform and remind – to create a single comprehensive reference covering the very complex task of planning a successful retirement.

About the Internet References
A word about the internet references - as Americans increasingly access the Internet at home and on their mobile devices, more and more companies and government agencies are providing content and product information on their websites, and information in paper form is slowly disappearing. In conjunction with this trend, you will find in this text many websites provided for gaining access to reference material, content, and contact information. If you do not have access to the internet, it may be helpful to find a friend or relative to assist you in finding and obtaining the required information.

Definition of Spouse
Throughout this book the use of the term "spouse" will be the legal definition used by and defined by federal law.

Chapter 1: Retire With Purpose

Retirement is a Journey, Not a Goal
Far too many people have the mistaken notion that if they can just get to retirement, all of their problems will just disappear and they will suddenly be happy; yet couldn't be farther from the truth, as retirement is a Journey, not a Goal. Consider the fact that you could be retired for 20 or 30 years, or even longer, roughly a full third of your life, and you now have a choice: you can struggle with uncertainty day to day and constantly react, or you can prepare and create the successful retirement that you have always dreamed about.

Building the Foundation
The foundation for a successful retirement is overall wellbeing, and will generally consist of balance and harmony in three critical areas of your life: Emotional, Physical, and Financial. Emotional wellbeing relates both to your psychological planning and preparedness leading up to your actual retirement, as well as your on-going emotional well-being throughout retirement. Physical Health is obvious: in order to enjoy a happy and active life during retirement, you will of course need to be in reasonably good health, as your retirement could last for twenty or more years. Finally, Financial Health is also obvious: it generally means that you have a plan that has removed the major uncertainties from your future, and that you are able to get comfortable with the money that you do have, regardless of the amount. Each of these components, then, are independent of each other, yet interdependent as well and it takes balance in all three areas combined to create overall wellbeing.

Emotional Wellbeing: Finding Happiness in Retirement

Making a successful transition from employment to retirement involves much more than selecting a date and attending that final Retirement Party. To be sure, it involves careful planning of finances, but it also includes a psychological/emotional transition, which is often overlooked, and begs the question: "has work become an addiction"? For some, perhaps not, but for many, or even most, spending your entire adult life in an environment structured with rules, deadlines, social order, and regular paychecks has become much more than a habit: a very subtle addiction, but an addiction nonetheless. Even for those who dislike their jobs, an abrupt termination without some careful consideration of both the reasons why you want to retire and what you will do after you retire could lead to some very strong feelings of loss, anxiety, unhappiness, and many times even depression. Ideally, you would create a comprehensive Retirement Life Plan, or at the very least, you should consider some in-depth discussions with a spouse or close friend, a mentor, or possibly even a psychologist, using the following series of questions as guideposts and topics for self-examination and consideration:

    a. Have I reached an age where everyone else seems to be retiring? Am I just going along with the crowd? Have I talked about it so long it has just become a self-fulfilling prophesy?

b. Do I want to retire merely because I hate my job or my boss? Would I consider continuing to work in some other position or with some other company if I was able to gain personal satisfaction and fulfillment?
c. Have I considered whether or not I will be happy living in an unstructured environment with no deadlines, no expectations, no time constraints, and no daily social interactions? While this sounds like nirvana from the working side of the street, the grass is not always greener, as the saying goes.
d. Is my personal identity tied to my job or my career, and if so, how will I fill this psychological vacuum?
e. Are my best friends and social circle all tied to my job or career? If I retire and they do not, how will I fill this psychological void?
f. How do I intend to occupy my time without my job to go to? Waking up every morning without an alarm and playing golf every day may sound ideal, but it can actually become boring, without a well-thought-out set of activities that will provide on-going and lasting meaning and fulfillment. Keep in mind that those retiring today at age 65 have a good chance of living to 100 or even older, meaning 35 or more years…almost as long as your entire working life.
g. Where do I plan to live, a decision I may not get to make on my own if I have a spouse or life partner, and a very important question to discuss.
h. If I have a spouse or partner, are they already retired, planning to retire, or planning to continue working? If already retired, how might the relationship change with both of you home, together, all day long? And if not retired, how will your new-found freedom impact their job responsibilities?

Creating a Retirement Life Plan

Creating a Retirement Life Plan starts with an evaluation of your current life situation by examining and assessing how satisfied you are with various aspects of your life. You can then move on to documenting your Vision for your life in retirement, a high level description of your hopes and dreams, of what you would like your life in retirement to look like and to be. Once you have completed your Vision, you can begin to gather specific details by reassessing and defining your values and your goals, then using that information as the foundation for exploring questions such as: What makes you happy? Why do you get up in the morning, or what would you like to have that would make you wake up excited and eager to begin each new day? What are you passionate about? How do you enjoy using your talents, and what is truly important to you? Being able to express your thoughts in writing can help you both clarify your thoughts and create a strong emotional foundation for entering this next phase of your life.

Creating Your Vision

A Vision Statement is a high-level declaration of your objectives and intentions; it is a picture of what you want your future to look like, the framework and inspiration for your life in retirement. Don't confuse the Vision Statement with a roadmap; it is not tied to the details, but it should be the compass for setting the direction for your life in retirement. Examples of

Vision Statement components would be: learn one or more new hobbies; work part-time doing something that I love; take more vacations; move to a warmer climate or a new location on a beach. These are declarations of your dreams, what you would like your retirement life to be, even if something doesn't seem possible at the moment (remember, in the early 1960s no one thought it would be possible to put a man on the moon until then President Kennedy gave us that challenge).

The Vision Statement, then, is high-level and conceptual; we can follow that by going a bit deeper, by reassessing and documenting our values and goals, and finally pulling it all together by creating our Retirement Life Plan.

Reassessing Values and Goals

We may have started our working career with a well thought-out set of goals and specific steps for achieving them, but life quickly intervenes: we end up working longer hours and weekends at times, we start a family and become immersed in our children's lives, with school and extra-curricular activities, with spouses (or partners), and aging parents; slowly many of our initial plans and goals seem to fade into the background while we continuously run on the treadmill of life, chasing the next big promotion and raise, and barely making time for ourselves. Yet retirement gives us both the time and the opportunity to take a step back, to re-evaluate our old goals and set new goals, while re-examining and clarifying our values.

Goals

The dictionary defines a goal as the end result of a person's effort; the object of what a person is striving for; a measurable outcome. In this case, it could be a broad, lifestyle change such as attaining a degree, learning a language, quitting smoking or becoming physically fit and healthy. It might also be the attainment of a dream, such as travel to a specific destination, or purchasing that lakefront property. Retirement represents a rare opportunity to define, redefine, reestablish or create new goals for yourself, yet there is nothing cast in concrete. If you start down a path and find you don't really like the direction, change it, and if you achieve a goal, replace it with another.

Values

Values, on the other hand, are a person's underlying principles or standards that drive their behavior; they have no start and end as do goals; they are ongoing, never ceasing. Examples of Values are: Compassion, Faith, Integrity, Honor, and Self-Esteem. It has been said that Goals give us a reason to wake up in the morning, and Values help us sleep at night.
Generally, we receive develop our values when growing up, from our parents, our teachers, and the teaching and guidance of our faith. Yet how many of us have ever taken the time to define our values by putting them in writing?

The Retirement Life Plan

As stated above, during our pre-retirement years our time, our focus, and our goals are centered on and around family, raising children, and work; often we have been so overwhelmed that we never took the time to formally understand what truly makes us happy and to formulate our life's goals. As we enter our retirement years, however, we now have an opportunity to take control of our future direction, to understand what motivates us and leaves us with an ongoing sense fulfillment and contentment. It even allows us to reinvent ourselves on many different levels. The Appendix Section has an exercise to assist us in this effort. You are encouraged to take this exercise seriously, as it could be the foundation for a happy and fulfilling life in retirement. Sit and ponder this alone, and share your thoughts and ideas with your spouse, partner, or closest friend.

The exercise has multiple parts:
1. Life Satisfaction Survey
2. Creating my Vision
3. Understanding and Defining what makes us happy
4. Understanding and Defining our Personal Values
5. Defining Our Initial Goals for Retirement
6. Creating our Retirement Life Plan

Each page will have a brief explanation and some examples to get you started. It may not seem as important as the money issues, but failure to consider the emotional aspects of retirement could lead to serious unhappiness and depression.

Physical Wellbeing: Lessons from the Blue Zones

It is just obvious that having good health in Retirement can make the difference between full enjoyment of your retirement years and a life plagued with illness and doctor appointments eating up all of your time, your resources, and eroding your mental and emotional happiness.

Some Tips from the Blue Zones

Blue Zones are the term for the five Demographic regions of the world where people commonly live active lives past the age of 100 years. The Blue Zone areas are Okinawa Japan; Sardinia Italy; the Nicoya Peninsula in Costa Rica; Ikaria Greece; and the Seventh-Day Adventists in Loma Linda California. In these Blue Zone areas, the researchers found that the people were generally happier and lived to 100 at a rate 10 times greater than in the United States, and coincidently they found that life in all the Blue Zones had many characteristics in common, including:

1. One of the best things you can do for emotional health is have a purpose, a reason to get up every morning and a reason to live. In the Blue Zones, they all have a purpose and they always put family first.
2. In the Blue Zones, aging is not about genes, it's about Lifestyle; they are not "couch potatoes, they walk everywhere, and they eat a healthy diet similar to the Mediterranean diet popular today.

3. People in the Blue Zones drink more water and eat less food; they drink at least two to three liters of water per day, and they pair that with a bit of red wine, one or two glasses. They do not drink heavy alcohol, sodas, or any other sugar-laden liquids. In terms of eating less: they usually eat a low calorie diet, some meat, but mostly vegetarian. Breakfast and lunch are the main meals of the day, with dinner light so as not to fall asleep on a full stomach. Finally, these centenarians eat only until they are 80% full.
4. They live a low stress lifestyle: they get plenty of sleep and rest; they are not run by the clock; and they make time for daily meditation or prayer.

Just Suggestions
Obviously this text is not meant to be a primer on Healthcare in retirement, however simply reading and thinking about the above tips from the Blue Zones will hopefully cause you to think about your own life and decide for yourself where you might want to make improvements in retirement.

Blue Zones

After discovering these various zones around the world, the researchers took out a map and circled each of the zones with a blue ink pen, and thus the name stuck. The most important lesson that the researchers found was that living longer relies on minimizing aging speed (obviously), and that the aging process can be accelerated or slowed down by the lifestyle that we choose. Most Americans, on the other hand, seem to always have their pedal to the floor.

For more information on the Blue Zones, see "The Blue Zones: Lessons for Living Longer from the People Who Live the Longest" by Dan Buettner,

---

Financial Wellbeing
The underlying foundation of a Successful Retirement is Happiness. Yet without that regular paycheck, continuous uncertainty about money can lead to nagging anxiety and even physical illness; and further, the most common cause of money insecurity in retirement is not knowing how much you have to spend, not keeping track of how much you do spend, and not knowing how long your money will last.

Planning is Essential
Keeping track of how much you have to spend, how much you do spend, and knowing how long your money will last starts with a documented spending plan; at the very least, knowing how much you have to spend from month to month and being able to make planning and spending decisions based on facts can eliminate uncertainty and the anxiety of not knowing. And at that point, if you find that you do not have sufficient money to meet all of your desires, you at least have the opportunity to decide for yourself: cut back on certain expenses or find some type of work for pay.

To assist you with this planning process, the Appendix Section of this book provides a Spending Plan template in workbook form. Knowing how much money you spend and how much income you anticipate is a great first step; a qualified Financial Advisor should then be able to assist you in crating income for life strategies.

In Summary

A successful retirement is much more than financial freedom; it involves physical health, along with finding opportunities and activities that create an ongoing sense of fulfillment and happiness. Spend some time planning and discussing with spouse, partner, or close friend; find/attend pre-retirement psychological classes or private counseling. Find and take an aptitude test and reinvent yourself; do the Retirement Life Plan exercise in the Appendix Section. Retirement may sound like the attainment of a lifelong goal, but without careful planning, could turn into years of anxiety and unhappiness.

Chapter 2: The Money Question?

The Money Question

The first and foremost question in everyone's mind focuses on money: how much will I need and can I create an income stream to last for the remainder of my life? Although the answer is going to depend on numerous factors, we can start with a general rule of thumb, which says that we will need 25 times our estimated annual expenses to support a withdrawal/investment strategy that will theoretically create a continuous income stream that we cannot outlive. This general concept relies on a 4% annual rate of withdrawal and sufficient portfolio growth to sustain this rate over 30 years or more. Again, this is merely a general rule of thumb, and does not take into account other issues such as inflation, taxes, and catastrophic emergency expenses, all of which will be addressed in the following sections.

A quick example would be as follows: you are looking for an income of $5,000 per month, $60,000 per year. According to the rule of thumb, you should have $1.5 million dollars in investment assets. The rule is linear, of course, meaning that it works for any desired income amount; if you are looking for $100,000 per year, you would need $2.5 million in investment assets to support that amount; looking for $50,000 per year, you would need $1.25 million, and etc.

Refining the Formula

In many cases we will have anticipated guaranteed income to cover a portion of our required income, such as Social Security, a Pension, an Annuity, or any other secure lifetime income source. In that case, we would subtract the anticipated income amount from the desired annual income to create a lesser base for calculating the required investible assets. Using the same desired $5,000 per month, for example, and anticipating a monthly Social Security payment of $2,500, would leave a shortfall of $2,500 per month, or $30,000 per year. Multiplying $30,000 times 25 now says that you should have $750,000 in investible assets to sustain your monthly desired income.

But Wait…

The above formula works well in theory, if our spending requirements remain constant over the rest of our lives, and there is never a market downturn to create negative growth and/or loss of principal, and further, what about the impact of inflation, taxes, and living too long? All are discussed in more detail below.

Longevity

The first impact on the potential longevity of your savings is your own longevity. Living a longer life is generally a good thing, but also means that your financial assets will need to last longer; and if your savings need to last longer, it could mean lowering your standard of living now, or potentially running out of money in the later stages of your life. Clearly, there are other factors involved in the calculation of the amount of money you will need, but the following table is presented merely to show the impact of this one factor alone:

Impact of Longevity Alone on the Total Amount needed to provide an income of $5,000/month
(Annual Investment Rate of Return = 6%)

Life Expectancy	Amount Required
15 Years	$ 595,000
20 Years	$ 700,000
25 Years	$ 779,000
30 Years	$ 835,000
35 Years	$ 880,000
Increase Needed	48%

Source: Social Security Administration

From the illustration above you can see the dramatic impact of the difference between living fifteen more years than thirty five more years – in effect, you would need almost Fifty Percent more money in your initial savings amount.

Inflation

Inflation is the increase in the price of goods and services year over year, which has the effect of diminishing your purchasing power over time. There are various reasons that cause inflation to occur, including an increase in wages demanded by workers year after year, and the amount of money that the government prints each and every year. The net result for each of us, however, is that prices do tend to go up, year after year.

For our purposes, let's look at a simple example: you go to the grocery store today and the total cost of all of the items in your shopping cart is $100. One year from now you return to the same store and purchase the same items, only this time, the cost is $105. This would be an increase due to inflation of 5 percent. If your income for that year rose 5 percent or more, you would not necessarily notice an impact, but if your income rose less than 5 percent, or you were on a fixed income, you might have to get by with one less item. And as time goes on, the impact of inflation can be quite substantial, as the chart illustrates:

	3%	4%
Current Year	$5,000	$5,000
10 Years	$6,720	$7,401
20 Years	$9.031	$10,956
30 Years	12,136	$16,217

Source: usinflationcalculator.com

Note: the **average annual** inflation rate over the past 30 years, using the Federal Government's Consumer Price Index, was 3.86%.

The Tricky Definition of Inflation
Initially, when the Government began to track Inflation, it was measured as the actual cost of maintaining a constant standard of living by measuring the price of a fixed basket of goods, year after year. At some point, however, the government removed food and energy from the calculation, deeming them too volatile and stating that price levels fail to persist over time.

Further, in the 1990s, the definition was changed again from actual cost of goods in the basket to a "constant level of satisfaction", a purely academic concept. The theory basically states that if the average household cannot stay ahead of the actual inflation rate, they will shift household preferences from more expensive items, like steak, for example, to less expensive products, like hamburger. The politicians were thus able to say that actual price increases "overstated inflation by not allowing for substitution", and thus, according to the politicians, the new approach was more accurate.

In reality, what this meant was a lowering of the cost of living adjustments for Social Security and other federal programs; it helped reduce deficit, and made then President Clinton look like a genius - and virtually all of the politicians went along with the new definition because no one in Congress had to vote in favor of actually lowering Social Security benefits.

CPI for Seniors
The government is currently calculating an experimental Consumer Price Index (CPI) for seniors 62 years of age and older. This index attempts to take into account the differences between the spending patterns of the elderly and the younger population, since the aged tend to spend a higher amount of their income on food consumed at home, on home heating, on household operation, and on medical care. They are much more likely to own mortgage-free homes and tend to spend less on restaurant meals, clothing, home furnishings, and recreation. At present, this is still in the experimental stages, however there has been talk in Congress about making the CPI for Seniors the basis for future Social Security Cost of Living adjustments.

Impact of Inflation
Over the past 30 years, the average annual inflation rate, as measured by the Government, is 3.86%. On the surface, this does not seem all that significant, but when you look at the actual impact of a 3% inflation rate on the amount of money required to maintain a $5,000 per month income over time, the effect becomes more obvious, as the following table illustrates.

Life Expectancy	Amount Required
15 Years	$ 730,000
20 Years	$ 900,000
25 Years	$1,052,000
30 Years	$1,183,000
35 Years	$1,300,000
Increase Needed	79.3%

Impact of Inflation and Longevity on the Total Amount needed to provide an income of $5,000/month
(Annual Investment Rate of Return = 6%)
Source: Extrapolated from Social Security Administration Table Above

Longevity + Inflation

From the illustration above you can see another dramatic impact: that of adding both living thirty five more years (versus only fifteen more years), plus the impact of a 3% rate of inflation over that same time period; now, you would need almost Eighty Percent more than your initial targeted savings amount.

Taxes

So far, we have ignored taxes in the above illustrations, merely to show the impact of each of the factors for illustration purposes. Like inflation, tax rates are subject to change at any time in the future, but one thing is for certain: there will be taxes, and taxes will further reduce the value of your nest egg. In general, tax rates will vary based on several factors including the type of income you receive, the type of account the income is coming from, and the number and type of any deductions that you might have. For our illustration, however, we will use an average tax bracket of 25 % and ignore all other factors, just to keep the example simple.

Life Expectancy	Amount Required
15 Years	$ 800,000
20 Years	$1,040,000
25 Years	$1,250,000
30 Years	$1,450,000
35 Years	$1,600,000
Increase Needed	100%

Impact of Longevity, Inflation, and Taxes on the Total Amount needed to provide an income of
$5,000/month (Annual Investment Rate of Return = 6%)
Source: Extrapolated from Social Security Administration Table Above

Summary: Longevity + Inflation+ Taxes

In summary, then, to maintain the purchasing power of $5,000 per month, given an estimated Investment Rate of Return of 6%, an Inflation Rate of 3%, and a Federal

Tax Rate of 25%, you would need an initial nest egg of slightly over $800 thousand dollars, if you expected to live 15 more years; but if you expected to live 35 more years, the total initial nest egg would need to be: $1.6 million, double the initial amount. The bottom line: the cumulative effect of all three of the above factors – Longevity, Inflation, and Taxes – is dramatic indeed and needs to be an integral component of any Financial Plan.

Other Risks to Consider
A final factor to consider has to do with both the Investment Rate of Return Risk along with the Sequence of Returns Risk. Both are further explained below:

Investment Rate Risk
The Investment Rate of Return is the average annual return provided by an investment (or cumulatively, all of your investments). This is a crucial assumption in creating a financial forecast, as well as a target that needs to be closely monitored year in and year out. The above illustrations assume that your investments will return at least 6% per year, year over year. Should your investments yield more, you have the option of giving yourself a raise for that year only, or saving and re-investing the excess to make up for any investment shortfalls in any of the following years. Will your Investment Rate of Return be constant year over year? Probably not, and further, depending on the types of investments you are employing, you could see large swings in the Investment Rate of Return each year: some years doing very well, some years even losing money. This is one of the main reasons for regularly monitoring your investment accounts and for meeting at least annually with your Financial Advisor, to ensure that you remain on target for continually meeting your goals.

Sequence of Returns Risk
As mentioned above, it is highly unlikely that your investments will produce the same Investment Returns, year over year, and further, some years could even see negative returns. During your retirement years, then, should a high proportion of negative returns occur in the beginning years, it will have a devastating overall effect and reduce the amount of income you can withdraw over your lifetime. This is called sequence of returns risk. The following tables illustrates this point: Starting off with $100,000, withdrawing 4% per year, with the annual return shown.

Principal	Income	Return	Principal	Income	Return
$100,000	$4,000	8%	$100,000	$4,000	-8%
$103,680	$4,147	10%	$88,320	$3,533	8%
$109,486	$4,379	12%	$91,570	$3,731	10%
$117,719	$4,709	10%	$96,698	$4,011	12%
$124,312	$4,972	-8%	$103,070	$4,236	10%
$109,792			$109,797		
Total	$22,207			$19,511	

As the table illustrates, negative returns early in your retirement years can have a drastic impact on your overall income throughout the remainder of your life. There are, however, potential strategies that can mitigate such impacts, and are discussed further in a later Chapter in this text.

In Summary

While all of the factors mentioned above can seem daunting, they are not necessarily insurmountable. It is highly recommended, then, that you find and work with a qualified and experienced Financial Advisor, one who can assist you in understanding and implementing some of the strategies that are described in detail in a later chapter entitled Making Your Money Last.

Cash Reserves

Generally, people are doing their financial planning and forecasting when they are enjoying relatively good health and are basing the budget projections on typical spending patterns. Somewhere down the road, however, they could encounter one or more major unplanned expenses: consider, for example, the high cost of a catastrophic illness, a new roof, or even a major automobile repair. For this reason, it is always financially prudent to factor in a cash reserve or an additional savings amount to cover any unforeseen future financial problems. Your Financial Advisor will be able to assist you in determining what your target Cash Reserve should be.

Chapter 3: Retirement Plans & Investment Accounts

Key Concepts
Before we begin, we will first identify and explain some important key terms that are common to most or all investment type accounts; further, these terms that will be used throughout this Chapter.

Beneficiary
In the financial world, a beneficiary typically refers to someone who is eligible to receive distributions from a life insurance policy, a Trust, or various other types of Investment and Retirement Accounts. Named beneficiaries will typically receive the money or ownership of the account immediately upon the death of the owner, without having to go through Probate or other legal processes. Without a named beneficiary, the money or ownership of the account will be distributed according to the terms of the decedent's *Will*, if one exists, or according to the laws of the state in which the decedent lived, if no *Will* existed. Many, but not all types of benefits will pass to a beneficiary tax-free.

Joint Ownership
In many cases, an investment account will be owned jointly, by two or more individuals. Legally, there are two types of joint ownership: Joint Tenants with Rights of Survivorship; and Tenants in Common. Both ownership types have been established to meet a different set of ownership needs, and both could have very different outcomes when one of the owners dies.

Joint Tenants with Rights of Survivorship
Joint Tenants with Rights of Survivorship (or JTWROS) is a type of ownership where two or more people jointly own an account, and where each of the owners has an equal right to the account's assets. In simple terms, when one spouse or owner dies, the surviving spouse or owner automatically assumes full ownership of the account, without having to go through Probate or other legal processes. This is, in effect, why many married couples choose this option for all of their Investment Accounts.

Joint Tenants in Common
The second type of joint ownership, and an alternative to JTWROS, is Joint Ownership as Tenants in Common. In this type of ownership, each spouse or owner owns a fixed percentage of the account, and if one owner dies, that owner's ownership share is passed to the owner's heirs through the *Will* and the Probate process. In a marriage, this type of ownership is typically established to ensure that children from a prior marriage will get funds from the decedent's portion of the account, although ownership could still pass to the surviving spouse if the deceased made such a provision in a *Will*.

Note of Caution
An additional note of caution: in most instances, Joint ownership of an account with a spouse, especially in a Community Property state, is completely normal, and, should one of the owners become incapacitated, or even die, the surviving owner would continue to have unrestricted access to the account. Joint ownership with children, relatives, or other friends, on the other hand, generally may not be a good idea, since any type of lawsuit or tax issue against one owner of an account will subject the entire account to that legal action. Further, if a joint owner (not a spouse) were to die, the deceased owner's half of the account might then become property of the deceased owner's family, which could cause serious problems if the sole intent was for one person (the deceased) to assist the original account owner with bill paying and managing the account. In these cases, it is preferable for the non-spousal party to have signature authority only (ie: if you need for them to pay bills, etc.) and further, include a Transfer on Death (see below) clause to allow them to immediately assume ownership after a death, generally without tax consequences. As always, you should seek the advice of a qualified financial professional for all questions regarding account ownership.

Transfer on Death
A Transfer on Death registration is a cost-free service that allows for the transfer of all stock, bond, and various other investment accounts to the person named in the agreement, upon the death of the account holder. Transfer on Death registration offers a quick and timely means of asset transfer and disbursement, as it completely avoids the probate process and can be activated simply by the presentation of a Death Certificate and proper identification. The person designated in the Transfer on Death registration is also known as the beneficiary.

Payable on Death
Very similar to Transfer on Death, a Payable on Death provision is a cost-free service that allows for the transfer of all checking and savings accounts, security deposits, savings bonds and other deposit certificates to the person named in the agreement, upon the death of the account holder. Just as Transfer on Death, Payable on Death provisions offer a quick and timely means of asset transfer and disbursement, as it completely avoids the probate process and can be activated simply by the presentation of a Death Certificate and proper identification. Generally speaking, you should consider having this provision in place with the name of the person that you want to receive the money formally on file for all of your bank accounts.

Investment Accounts

In general, this type of account is held by an Individual, or jointly with one or more individuals, for the purpose of investing in various Stocks, Bonds, Mutual Funds, and other types of investment products. This type of account is typically held at a brokerage firm or a bank; funds may be freely added or withdrawn from the account, generally without restrictions. Taxation occurs at year-end in the form of Capital Gains and Capital Loss, according to the current tax statutes.

Retirement Accounts

Retirement accounts are a special type of investment for depositing, maintaining, and accumulating money for retirement. There are various types of Retirement Accounts: some held and maintained individually, some sponsored and managed by an employer. The following sections provide an overview of the most common types of Retirement Accounts. Note that the information below provides only general account provisions, which may be different for specific plans.

Individual Retirement Accounts

IRA Accounts

The term IRA stands for Individual Retirement Account, of which there are two types: a Traditional IRA and a Roth IRA.

Traditional IRA

A Traditional IRA is a type of tax deferred Retirement Savings Account, where the owner deposits money into an account held by a custodian, typically a Financial Institution or Retail Brokerage firm. Tax deferred means that all of your interest, dividends, and capital gains will grow and compound free of federal income taxes. Traditional IRAs come in two varieties: deductible and non-deductible, where deductible means that the amount of money deposited is deducted from the owner's gross income prior to calculating the taxes due each year. Whether you are eligible for a full or partial deduction, or no deduction at all, depends on your income and whether you are covered by or have access to a retirement account through your employer. The contribution and deduction limits are set by the IRS and are subject to change annually.

Since taxes were generally not paid on all (or a portion) of the original contributions or the growth of the investments (both deductible and non-deductible IRA), taxes will be due as the funds are withdrawn, typically after retirement., and all withdrawals are subject to Ordinary Income Tax rules (as opposed to Capital Gains rules). Further, withdrawals are generally not allowed before the owner's age of 59½ without a substantial tax penalty (currently 10%), although there are certain circumstances, such as disability or death, which allow distributions prior to age 59½ without the tax penalty. Once again, these rules are set by the IRS and subject to change. If you have questions about your specific situation, you should seek the guidance of a qualified Financial Advisor, CPA, or Tax Advisor.

Generally speaking, the Traditional IRA is available to and opened by an individual, on their own. Additionally, there are other types of IRA accounts that can be opened by self-employed individuals and small business owners, among them the SEP IRA and the SIMPLE IRA. Once again, for questions about your specific situation, you should seek the guidance of a qualified Financial Advisor, CPA, or Tax Advisor.

Taking Money from an IRA

Generally speaking, while you can begin taking qualified withdrawals from a Traditional IRA after age 59½, you <u>must</u> start taking withdrawals beginning April 1 of the year following the year that you reach 70½. These are known as "Required Minimum Distributions" (sometimes referred to as RMDs), and the amount of the distribution will depend on both the total amount in the account and your life expectancy, according to specific tables published by the IRS.

Roth IRA Accounts

Like a Traditional IRA, a Roth IRA is also a type of Retirement Savings Account, where the owner deposits money into an account held by a custodian, typically a Financial Institution or Retail Brokerage. Unlike a Traditional IRA, however, money deposited into a Roth IRA is done with after-tax dollars, meaning that you have already paid the income taxes on this money. What is distinctive about a Roth IRA, then, is that the money inside the account accumulates and can potentially be withdrawn entirely tax-free, as long as certain conditions are met. Also, unlike Traditional IRAs, Roth IRAs are not subject to mandatory Required Minimum Distributions, but like Traditional IRAs, there is currently a 10% penalty for early withdrawal, prior to age 59½.

Criteria for Tax-Free Roth IRA Distributions

Funds withdrawn from a Roth IRA will be completely tax-free to the owner as long as the following criteria are met:

- The distribution is made after five years from the date when the account was first opened; and

- The distribution is made after you reach age 59½, or because you are disabled, or to purchase a home for the first time, or paid to a beneficiary after a death.

Note: since deposits into a Roth IRA are paid with post-tax dollars (tax has already been paid), there is no requirement for taking Required Minimum Distributions from a Roth IRA Account.

Employer Pension & Retirement Accounts

Defined Contribution Plans
A Defined Contribution Plan is the legal term for a plan in which an employee's retirement income benefits depend solely on the contributions made to the account by the employee, and the investment performance of the assets in their account. Typically, the employee has control over how the contributions to their plan are invested and may generally include stocks (often including company stock), bonds, and various other investment vehicles. Examples of defined-contribution plans include 401(k) plans, 403(b) plans, and 457 plans, all of which share similar characteristics. For the purpose of brevity, we will use only the term 401(k) when referring to Defined Contribution Plans throughout the text – it is understood to refer to all forms of the Defined Contribution Plans.

Defined Benefit Plans
A defined-benefit plan is the formal name for a company Pension Plan; in its simplest terms, it is an employer-sponsored retirement plan set up to pay retiring employees a portion of their salary for the remainder of their lives. The program is completely funded and managed by the employer, and benefits are generally computed using a formula that considers several factors such as age, length of employment and salary history. The company administers the investment portfolio and all investment risk is borne by the employer.

Senior Investor Concerns

Senior Investor Defined
The U.S. Securities and Exchange Commission (SEC) generally defines a Senior Investor as someone already retired or nearing retirement, and can generally be assumed to be someone 50 years of age or older. This is the definition that will be used throughout the remainder of this section when referring to a Senior Investor.

Senior Investor Concerns
Securities Regulators have begun to explore the problem of elder financial abuse that can arise from a combination of an aging baby boomer population, complex financial products and retirement nest eggs that are attractive to scammers. Consider that approximately 75% of America's consumer financial assets, an estimated $16 trillion, are held by households headed by someone who is 50 years old or older. This is truly a staggering statistic, which could tempt less than honest brokers to take advantage of elderly client's trust and forgetfulness.

Conversely, even honest brokers are now faced with serious problems when attempting to communicate with clients who suffer from memory problems, diminishing cognitive capacity, or outright elder abuse by family, relatives, or friends. Meanwhile, the honest advisors can struggle to determine exactly what to do to properly advise their elderly clients who forget facts, dates, conversations, and who might ask their advisors to help them with unwise or risky investment transactions.

Source: Protecting Senior Investors:
http://www.sec.gov/spotlight/seniors/seniorspracticesreport092208.pdf
(As of 3-19-2015)

Major Risk Considerations

As the baby boomer population ages, one of the most critical issues has become diminished mental capacity, which would leave them susceptible to outright financial abuse, or simply the sale of generally unsuitable products for the sake of a commission by inexperienced or less-than-diligent brokers. This is, in fact, the very issue that the SEC and the industry in general are attempting to address. More specifically, seniors, as a group, require a more carefully thought-out strategy than the younger investor, due to their dramatically different financial and life goals; in general this means:

- Shortened Investment Time Horizons
- Reduced Risk Tolerance
- Increased Dependence on Liquidity

Realize, for example, that while a 30 year old investor may be able to recover from a double-digit market drop or year-after-year rising inflation, senior investors have fewer options and either factor can be financially disastrous.

Finally, watching inflation or other factors erode their standard of living might cause a senior investor to reach for higher returns at the risk of investment quality, requiring extended diligence and comprehensive guidance on the part of their financial advisors.

Only Line of Defense

The best, and virtually only line of defense for Senior Investors is a consortium of concerned and vigilant family, friends, and caregivers, in the form of:

- Carefully watching for early signs of diminished mental capacity or dementia
- Reviewing Investment Proposals for Suitability Concerns
- Having and maintaining their "Affairs" package up to date and in order

Senior Investor Summary

The reward for taking on risk is the potential for a greater investment return. On the other hand, lower risk investments, although accompanied by generally lower returns, are generally more appropriate for a Senior Investor counting on the income from the investment to support them in retirement. To assist you in determining your own personal Risk Tolerance, there are numerous websites with questionnaires to help you sort through and come to a general understanding of the amount of risk that it would be prudent for you to take. Yet an even better option might be to seek the assistance and advice from a qualified Financial Advisor who can provide you with the most accurate insight and guidance tailored to your specific needs, requirements, and life situation. For more information on finding a qualified Financial Advisor, please see the Chapter entitled: Hiring Professional Advisors.

> **Have You Noticed Any of These Warning Signs?**
> The Alzheimer's Association has a web site with excellent explanation of:
> - Dementia
> - Alzheimer's
> - Early Onset Dementia and Alzheimer's
> - Stages
> - Risk Factors
> - Checklist of signs and symptoms to watch for
>
> www.alz.org/alzheimers_disease_1973.asp
>
> www.alz.org/national/documents/checklist_10signs.pdf

Smart Retirement

Chapter 4: Lifetime Income Strategies

The Money Question Again

As mentioned in earlier chapters, the first and foremost question in everyone's mind is money: how much will I need, do I have enough, and is there a strategy to create an income stream to last for the remainder of my life? Although the answer again is going to depend on numerous factors, and while it is virtually impossible to create guarantees against every eventuality, there are strategies that theoretically and statistically will create a continuous unending income stream. Please note that: a) the strategies are hypothetical and dependent on unpredictable future returns of the stock market; and/or b) Annuity guarantees are dependent on the ongoing claims paying ability of the issuing Insurance Company.

Smart Buckets: Basic Components

The Smart Buckets Strategy was assembled by the author, in conjunction with several prominent fund managers and expert strategists, and utilizes the following key elements:

1. Three* Allocation "buckets":
   - A Protected Current Spending Bucket
   - A Conservative Intermediate Bucket
   - An Aggressive Growth Bucket
2. Investment funds with built-In Stop-Loss Protection mechanisms

Note: that the Strategy can utilize more than three buckets for a move complex situations, however the operational concept is the same regardless of the number of buckets required.

The strategy requires the following components:
- Desired Annual Income Amount;
- Estimated Income from Known Sources;
- Total Investable Assets;
- Income Shortfall; and
- Income Stability Ratio.

The Desired Annual Income should be more than a guess, and requires some homework using a format like the Spending Plan Template provided in the Appendix Section. This template will help in uncovering and documenting all expected/anticipated weekly, monthly, and/or annual expenses to provide a more accurate Income picture for a full year.

The Estimated Income from Known Sources is the total of all permanent, life-long income and will typically include Social Security Payments, Pension Payments, Annuity Payments, and etc.; these are payments that are generally expected to last a lifetime. These guaranteed income payments provide the floor, or a solid income foundation that we can depend on, and that is not subject to the volatility of the stock market. More about this topic in a later paragraph.

The Total Investable Assets are the sum total of all the assets from your 401(k) (or other Retirement Savings account such as 403(b), and etc.), your IRAs, your Investment Accounts, Savings Accounts, and etc. In short, all available funds that can be gathered together and used to fund the Smart Buckets.

In most cases, the Desired Annual Income will be larger than the total Estimated Income from Known Sources, meaning that we will need to rely on our Investable Assets to make up the difference. Subtracting the Income from Known Sources from the Desired Annual Income will give us the Income Shortfall. (If you are one of the few fortunate people who already have more permanent Income from Known Sources, you can probably skip the remainder of this Section and focus on structuring your Investable Assets for mitigating potential catastrophic healthcare risks as well as safeguarding the assets for leaving a legacy to your heirs).

One additional component needs to be calculated and that is the Income Stability Ratio; this ratio is calculated by dividing total Estimated Income from Known Sources by the Desired Annual Income. This gives us a snapshot of the percentage of our total Investable Assets that will be relied upon to produce the Income Shortfall for an indefinite basis.

At this point, an example might be helpful: let's assume, for example, that, after calculating all of the expenses for a single year, we discover that we will need $60,000 per year, each and every year, for living expenses. Let's also assume that we will have $30,000 per year in permanent, life-long income. Subtracting the total Estimated Income from Known Sources from the Desired Annual Income leaves us with an Income Shortfall of $30,000. Further, by dividing the Estimated Income from Known Sources by the Desired Annual Income gives us an Income Stability Ratio of 50%. This tells us that we will have to rely on the stock market for 50% of all our future income, and this is where we will employ the Smart Buckets Strategy. *Please note that an additional assumption of this Strategy is that the Total Investable Assets is large enough to generate reasonable returns without needing to resort to high risk investment strategies in the Aggressive Growth Bucket.*

Smart Buckets Strategy Overview

In its simplest terms, the Smart Continuous Pay Strategy works as follows: Starting with the Income Shortfall from above, we allocate three years of Income Shortfall to the Protected Current Spending Shortfall Bucket; this Bucket is invested in very safe Fixed Income investment funds such as Money Market, short term Bonds and Notes, US Treasuries, and etc. This ensures that there will always be three years of income available to meet our projected living expenses, regardless of market performance. Additionally, we have selected three years for this Bucket since historically, the market has never been down for three consecutive years.

All remaining Investable Assets are divided equally into a Conservative Intermediate Bucket and an Aggressive Growth Bucket. The Conservative Intermediate Bucket is invested in fixed income assets such as Corporate Bonds and Preferred Stocks that pay consistent dividends with very little growth. This fund is intended to provide small but stable annual increases targeted to at least keep ahead of inflation and to not lose value. The Aggressive Growth Bucket is invested in growth equities (stocks and stock funds) with the target of creating a larger return over the long run. There is generally more risk to these types of equities, but over time they have proven to provide better than average returns.

Additionally, we have a safeguard feature built in to the Buckets Strategy. Certain fund managers have incorporated various Stop Loss protection schemes into their funds that will constantly monitor the fund and automatically move everything to cash if the fund suffers a relatively small, pre-determined amount of loss; this approach is in place to prevent catastrophic losses such as occurred in 2000 and 2008. While only a very few funds today offer this type of protection, the Smart Buckets Strategy will only use funds that employ this type of protection.

Smart Buckets Strategy: Follow the Money

Operationally, the Strategy works as follows: starting with the first year of operation, and continuing each consecutive year, funds are withdrawn from the Protected Current Spending Bucket for use in meeting ongoing spending needs. At the end of each year, the withdrawal from the Protected Current Spending Bucket is replaced with funds from the Conservative Intermediate Bucket, and further, the funds withdrawn from the Conservative Intermediate Fund are replaced with funds from the Aggressive Growth Bucket. In years with sufficient gains in the Conservative Intermediate Fund and/or the Aggressive Growth Bucket, additional money may be transferred to the Protected Current Spending Fund to help offset inflation. In years where there is insufficient market gain to fully replace the Current Spending Bucket or the Conservative Intermediate Bucket, transfers may be suspended until the market regains its momentum.

Smart Buckets: Operational Example

Assume that we need $30,000 per year income from our Total Investable Assets to cover annual Income Shortfall, and that we have $500,000 in Total Investable Assets from our 401(k):
   a. Three years of Income equals $90,000, so this amount is moved into our Protected Current Spending Bucket
   b. The remaining $410,000 is moved into the Conservative Intermediate Bucket and the Aggressive Growth Bucket
   c. The minimum target growth rate for the Conservative Intermediate Bucket would be 3% (at a minimum to keep up with inflation)
   d. The minimum target growth rate for the Aggressive Growth Bucket would be 7.5% to create at least an additional $30,000 income replacement per year.
   e. Statistically, this Strategy should continue to produce at least the current required income amount indefinitely, since the average annualized return of the S&P 500 over the past 90 years has been 9.8%; the market has tended to expand over longer periods of time, and lastly, there has never been a negative market three years in a row.

Once again, it is necessary to point out that this illustration is completely hypothetical based on historical returns, and of course, past performance is no guarantee of future results.

Smart Bucket Strategy Summary

This strategy has been designed to generate a continuous income stream that theoretically and statistically could last indefinitely. The Strategy is, of course, hypothetical in nature, and while historical results predict the high degree of success of this Strategy, the future is completely dependent on unpredictable future returns of the stock and bond markets, and further, on the U.S. and global economic and political stability.

Flooring Options: Expanding the Foundation

As mentioned above certain sources of income are stable and guaranteed for life; they include sources such as Social Security and employer pensions. Additionally, various insurance products can be used to provide additional guaranteed* income to strengthen the foundation. The use of these products is generally referred to as Flooring, and the products generally include certain types of Annuities, and certain types of Cash Value Life Insurance. Both are explained in further detail below.

Annuities with Guaranteed Income

Insurance Companies offer various types of Annuities with lifetime income guarantees* that can be the equivalent of your own private pension plan. Yet over the years, Annuities have gained an incredibly bad reputation, and deservedly so based on how they have been marketed and sold to the public. In order to better understand Annuities and why they should not be overlooked as a Retirement Income Strategy, and to assist you in making a better informed decision, the following Issues and Benefits are discussed in detail:

Annuity Issues:
The biggest issues with Annuities are a general confusion in trying to understand the policy and its various rider options, the high fees charged by the Insurance Company, the high commission paid to the advisor, and the Early Surrender Charges:

   a. Annuities are complex insurance products with numerous rider options, and are extremely confusing to understand even by many of the advisors who sell them; further, there is a general misunderstanding about the values in the investor's Principal Bucket and Income Benefit Bucket.
   b. Annuities generally pay the advisor a large, upfront commission, which can selfishly motivate some advisors to sell this type of investment over cheaper, more suitable alternatives
   c. The insurance company charges several types of fees to administer the product, and further, if the product is a Variable Annuity, each Mutual Fund in the underlying Product Mix will also charge a management fee.

d. The Annuity Income Guarantee, once activated, will generally remain fixed for the remainder of a person's life, and does not provide for increases to cover increases in the cost of living resulting from inflation
e. Lastly, there is generally a holding period of, on average, seven to ten years; this means that should the investor want to withdraw the balance, an early withdrawal penalty or Surrender Charge will be assessed.. The Insurance Company will generally impose a decreasing Surrender Charge over the Surrender Period, such as: 10% first year, 8% second year, 6% third year, etc., down to 0% after the end of the Surrender Period.

Potential Annuity Benefits

Annuities, on the other hand, when properly used for the purpose of creating a Retirement Income Foundation that cannot be outlived, can be a powerful component of the overall Retirement Income Strategy. Benefits of an annuity when used in this manner include:

a. The Income Benefit will pay the contract holder a guaranteed income for life*
b. Money in the annuity grows tax deferred, free of annual capital gains taxes; taxes are not owed until money is withdrawn.
c. The Income Benefit generally grows year over year at a guaranteed rate, regardless of market performance of the associated index or underlying mutual funds, until the Income Benefit is activated (ie: begin receiving regularly scheduled income payments); further, while the Income Benefit is still growing, the Income Benefit amount can receive a step-up increase over and above the guaranteed rate if the associated index or underlying mutual funds experience an exceptionally good rate of return.
d. Once your Income Benefit is activated (you begin taking regularly scheduled monthly payments) that income is guaranteed for the rest of your life*. The income is, of course, drawn from your funds in your Principal Account, however, should your Principal Account become depleted (goes to zero) the Insurance Company will continue to pay the monthly income for the rest of your life; in effect, you are purchasing insurance against outliving your money.
e. Most annuities today have a standard Death Benefit, meaning that any money not paid out in the form of an Income Benefit will go to your heirs at your death. Additionally, some companies even offer a non-declining Death Benefit, meaning that if any money remains in the account at the time of the contract holder's death, the entire original principal amount will be paid to the heirs.

Understanding Annuities: Recap

Annuities are a Retirement Income product, not an investment product. This is a very important point to understand. You should only consider purchasing an annuity if:

a. You want to create an income stream guaranteed for life*, as part of a Retirement Income Strategy.

b. The income stream from the annuity will be substantial.
   c. You understand that the income payments generated from the annuity will generally be fixed for the remainder of your life
   d. You understand that the money invested in the annuity will not be available to you, even in an emergency, in any other form but income stream, and that withdrawing money apart from the intended income stream will both reduce all future income and potentially invalidate any guarantees.
   e. The annuity is generally part of an overall Retirement Income Strategy created by a qualified and experienced Financial Advisor.

   All guarantees are completely dependent on the ongoing claims paying ability of the issuing Insurance Company.

7702 Plan Accounts

7702 is the IRS Tax Code Number for this specific type of Indexed Universal Life Insurance (IUL) contract specifically designed to create tax free lifetime income in retirement coupled with a life insurance death benefit. These plans are further detailed in the following Chapter.

Chapter Summary

Either the Smart Buckets Strategy alone, or coupled with the some type of Income Flooring Strategy, has the potential to turn your nest egg into an income stream that has the potential to last you for the rest of your life, with the further potential of ongoing growth to keep up with inflation. These strategies and products, however, can be extremely complex: please seek the advice and guidance of a qualified Financial Advisor, with experience in constructing life-long income from their clients hard-earned Retirement Savings, if you are interested in utilizing this type of strategy. If you do not already have one, or would like a second opinion, please feel free to contact the author at by email or phone listed on the first page of this book.

Chapter 5: Tax Free Retirement Income

"Anyone may so arrange his affairs that his taxes shall be as low as possible; he is not bound to choose that pattern which will best pay the Treasury; there is not even a patriotic duty to increase one's taxes" Judge Learned Hand, Federal Judge

Tax-Free Lifetime Income: The Gold Standard

"I don't have a crystal ball but it wouldn't surprise me if taxes went up in the future given the current deficit, underfunding of Social Security and longevity of today's retirees" Everyone

Taxes: The Ticking Time Bomb

The steep economic downturn and massive coronavirus rescue spending will nearly quadruple the fiscal 2020 U.S. budget deficit to a record $3.8 trillion, bringing the U.S. Treasury's official figure for the debt of the United States government on April 23, 2020 is $24.7 trillion (and growing). This is a staggering amount, considering that just 10 years ago the federal debt was about $12 Trillion, and twenty years ago it was $5 Trillion with an overall budget surplus that year; and further, by the end of 2020, interest alone on the debt is estimated to be $1 Trillion. So the overriding question is "how are we going to pay for it"? Consider the following table of Total Debt, Debt as a percentage of GDP (Gross Domestic Product: the total market value of all finished goods and services produced in the country for a given year), and Total Tax Revenue for the given year:

Year	Total Federal Debt	Percent of GDP	Total Tax Revenue
2000	$ 5 Trillion Dollars	55%	$2.03 Trillion
2010	$12 Trillion Dollars	99%	$2.16 Trillion
2020	$25 Trillion Dollars*	107%	$3.46 Trillion**

*Federal Debt Figure as of April 2020 and climbing

**Revenue Figure as of Dec 31, 2019, with massive unemployment due to the Coronavirus will mean potentially lower Tax Revenue in 2020

Source: www.thebalance.com/national-debt-by-year-compared-to-gdp-and-major-events-3306287; www.thebalance.com/current-u-s-federal-government-tax-revenue-3305762

Who Is Going to Pay?

Retirees are sitting right in the hot seat: baby boomers have now reached their peak earning years and are going into their retirement years with total retirement assets of $29.1 Trillion as of March 31, 2019* and in thirty years, as the last of the baby boomers dies off and the next generation is retired, total retirement assets are expected to be a whopping $68 Trillion. At this point, there are really only two choices: raise taxes or suffer massive run-away inflation**. In either case, those on a fixed income, especially Retirees could be impacted the hardest, as they will have been out of the workforce for several years and either cannot or are physically unable to go back to work.

*Source: Invesco.us.com

**It is the responsibility of the FED to control the Money Supply and also keep a lid on inflation; without additional tax revenue, the FED will be forced to "print" more money, but that much more money in circulation will have the effect of devaluing the dollar; as an example think of gold; it is valuable because it is rare, but if we were to find gold pebbles and rocks everywhere we looked, it would significantly lose its value.

Three Types of Retirement Savings Accounts
There are three general categories of retirement savings accounts:
- Taxable Today
- Tax Deferred
- Tax Free

Taxable Today accounts include Personal Savings and Investment Accounts; typically, these accounts will receive a form 1099 at the end of each year, and either Ordinary Income or Capital Gains taxes will need to be annually.

Tax Deferred accounts generally include Traditional Employer Sponsored Savings programs (ie: 401(k), 403(b), SEP, SIMPLE, and etc.), Individual Retirement Accounts (IRA), and Annuities. Tax Deferred means that no taxes are assessed during the accumulation phase, as the account grows due to interest and investment gains; then, at retirement, taxes will be paid on each dollar taken from the account, at the then current tax rate (which could be at higher rates year after year as the tax rates change).

Tax Free accounts generally include Roth Employer Sponsored Savings programs (ie: Roth 401(k), 403(b), etc.), Roth Individual Retirement Accounts (Roth IRA), and Lifetime Collateral Accounts (a very specific form of Cash Value Life Insurance structured to create tax free income in retirement). These accounts are funded with post-tax dollars meaning that Ordinary Income Tax has been paid on the funds prior to being deposited into the account; the funds then grow tax exempt due to interest and investment gains; and finally, at retirement the funds can be withdrawn tax free. Additionally, Municipal Bonds also fall into the category of Tax Free accounts; they are purchased with post-tax dollars and interest from the bonds comes to you tax free.

Taxes in Retirement
Aside from certain investments within individual investment accounts that are taxed at Capital Gains tax rates, all other distributions from Taxable and Tax Deferred accounts are taxed at Ordinary Income rates; currently, both the Capital Gains rate and the Ordinary Income rate are relatively low, compared to rates in the past; these rates are adjusted periodically by Congress, with the current low rates set to be expire at the end of year 2025. At that point, it is likely that the deficit will have increased even more, and that Congress will have no choice to significantly raise taxes across the board.

Smart Retirement

Table of Taxes in Retirement Income Sources (on Withdrawal of funds)

Income Source	Taxable	Contrib Limits	RMD	Impact Medicare	Could Lose Value
Social Security	Yes*	n/a	n/a	No	**
Pension	Yes	Yes	No	Yes	No
Traditional 401(k), etc.	Yes	Yes	Yes	Yes	Yes
Traditional IRA	Yes	Yes	Yes	Yes	Yes
Individual Savings/Investments	Yes	No	No	Yes	Yes
Annuity	Yes	No	Yes*	Yes	No
Municipal Bonds	No	No	No	Yes	Yes
Roth 401(k), etc.	No	Yes	No	Yes	Yes
Roth IRA	No	Yes	No	Yes	Yes
7702 Plan	No	No	No	No	No

*Up to 85% could be taxed depending on total income

Impact of Taxes on Retirement Income

Note: all numbers in the following example are hypothetical. In this hypothetical example, we will use Debbi and David are twins; both are in the 30% average tax rate; both want to have $100,000 per year in retirement income from their various retirement savings accounts. All of Dan's income sources are in tax deferred accounts. Note: all numbers below are completely hypothetical, and are presented in a fashion so as to make the point clear.

When Dan takes $100,000 out of his accounts each year, he will owe the government $30,000 in taxes and only realize $70,000 in actual income each year. With a life expectancy of 20 years, that means that Dan will have to pay $600,000 in income taxes. Additionally, if Dan wanted to have the full $100,000 in income to spend after taxes, he would have to increase his withdrawal amount to about $144,000 from his accounts; over a 5 year period he would have depleted his accounts by $720,000 to achieve $500,000 in income to him.

And lastly, if Dan is relying rely on the stock market to ensure that he will not run out of money in his lifetime, massive losses in the market like those experienced in the 2000 and 2008 market crashes could cause him to run out of money too soon, or seriously impact his standard of living in his later years.

Contrast with Tax Free Income in Retirement

Debbi, on the other hand, has all of her retirement savings in an account that will produce tax free income; that means that Debbi will have the full $100,000 to spend each year without owing any federal taxes, and over, 5 years, Debbi will have had

$500,000 to spend, and if properly set up in the right vehicles, her income would be stable for the rest of her life.

Municipal Bonds

For investors seeking tax-advantaged investing, municipal bonds and municipal bond mutual funds offer a potential solution. Municipal bonds are issued and backed by city, county, state, and other municipal authorities seeking to raise capital for public projects, such as transportation infrastructure, schools, utilities, toll roads, or other improvements, and pay interest on a periodic basis. Their chief appeal is that the interest payments that these fixed-income investments generate are typically exempt from federal taxes, so they can help an investor reduce income-tax bills. There are certain risks, however, with investing in municipal bonds:

- **Risk of Default and Loss of Capital.** All investments carry risk, and municipal bonds are no different; historically, it's been somewhat rare, however we are now at a point where virtually every major city, county, and state have massive unfunded and underfunded liabilities, chief among them are the pension liabilities; should an issuer go bankrupt, interest payments and principal would be lost.
- **Interest Rate Risk.** When interest rates go up, current bonds lose value, since older bonds carry that a lower interest rate must be sold at a discount to equal current bond yields. This is less of a concern if you have individual bonds plan to hold the bonds to maturity, but frequently happens with bond mutual funds in times of rising interest rates.
- **Bond Yields May Not Beat Inflation.** Because municipal bonds offer tax advantages, their yields tend to be relatively low, and therefore unlikely to beat inflation over an extended period of time.

Roth IRA and Roth 401(k) Accounts

Similar to a 7702 Plan Account, contributions to a Roth IRA and/or a Roth 401(k) account are post-tax, meaning that the tax has already been paid before the contribution is made. The Roth funds are then invested in various Mutual Funds (or other qualified investment vehicles); the grow tax free, and lastly, funds are also tax free when withdrawn.

While tax-free growth, and tax-free withdrawals are outstanding benefits, Roth accounts also have some major disadvantages, including:

- Contributions invested in Mutual Funds (and other investment vehicles) are subject to Market Volatility and could lose substantial value, such as approximately 40% or more during the 2000 Dot Com Bubble Burst and the 2008 Sub-Prime Mortgage Meltdown.
- The Federal Government limits the contributions to both the Roth IRA and the Roth 401(k), and in some cases, prohibits contributions to a Roth IRA if the person makes over a certain income threshold.

7702 Plans

7702 is the IRS Tax Code Number for this specific type of Indexed Universal Life Insurance (IUL) contract specifically designed to create tax free lifetime income in retirement coupled with a life insurance death benefit. This is done in two phases: the accumulation phase and the distribution phase. During the accumulation phase funds are allocated to an Equity Index account, where your account is credited annually based on the performance of one of the major stock market indexes, such as the S&P 500, etc. A key feature here is that your money is not invested in in the stock market, merely credited based on gains in the particular market index, meaning that in down years, your account will simply not be credited, not lose value; to repeat, your account will never have a loss due to negative stock market returns; if the index goes down instead of up, no interest is credited to your account.

Premium payments are generally paid periodically, with growth over a number of years, or a single, large, one time premium, held in an interest-bearing reserve account and applied over a fixed period of years.

Advantages of a 7702 Plan (IUL) Account

- **Less Risk:** As stated above, the funds are not directly invested in the stock market, they are generally less risky than other stock market investments.
- **Cash Value Accumulation:** Amounts credited to the cash value grow tax deferred, and over time, as the cash value grows, the cash value can pay the insurance premiums, giving the policyholder the option to reduce or stop making out-of-pocket premium payments at some future point.
- **Death Benefit:** Because this is a life insurance product, there is an associated death benefit; this benefit is not subject to income or death taxes, and will not be required to go through probate.
- **Distribution:** The cash value in IUL insurance policies can be accessed at any time without penalty, regardless of a person's age.
- **Unlimited Contribution**: IUL insurance policies have no IRS limitations on annual contributions.
- **No Impact on Medicare Premiums:** Income from this IUL policy is considered a loan, so income taken from this policy will not cause increases in Medicare Premiums
- **No RMD Requirements:** Unlike Traditional Retirement Savings programs like Traditional IRAs and Traditional 401(k)s, there are no mandatory Required Minimum Distributions
- **Additional Chronic and Terminal Illness Benefits:** Many policies allow access to a portion or all of the Death Benefit in case of Chronic Illness (needing Long Term Care) or Terminal Illness

Note: all guarantees are dependent on the claims paying ability of the issuing company.

Considerations in Choosing a 7702 Plan (IUL) Account

- **Caps on Accumulation Percentages:** Insurance companies generally set a maximum annual caps on the participation rate that is less than 100%.

- **Based on an Equity Index**: If the index is negative for the year, no interest is credited to the cash value; as stated above, the goal of an IUL is to profit from upward movements in the index.
- **Severe Penalty for Early Termination**: the policies are generally intended to be a retirement income savings plan or a replacement for a college saving plan; as such, they are expected to be in effect for at least 10-15 years, and typically will have a substantial penalty for cancelling the policy within the first 10-12 years; this means that should you change your mind for any reason during the surrender period, you will receive less back than the total premiums paid; after the surrender period, the cash value will generally be the same as or exceed the total premiums paid.
- **Fees**: the insurance company charges fees for administrating and managing the product, as well as for the providing and overseeing the death benefit.

In summary, 7702 Plan Accounts are one of the only available investment vehicles that can provide both a tax free income stream in retirement as well as a death benefit that is tax free to your beneficiaries. They can be used to create a stand-alone Retirement Income Plan, or in combination with your employer's 401(k) plan, investing anything over the amount that your employer will match in a 7702 Plan Account. Lastly, these accounts are complex insurance products and require guidance and planning assistance from a true Financial Advisor, one who is a Fiduciary, and has the training, background, and licenses to take into account your entire retirement goals and needs, and structure the best possible plan for you, utilizing your complete financial picture.

> **Note**: Missing the 40 worst days in the SP 500 Index during a 20-year period (through 2019) would have increased investment returns by nearly 991% as compared to a buy-and-hold strategy; This is a major benefit of a 7702 Plan sine your principal not invested in the stock market.

Best of Both Worlds
One way to receive substantially all of your income in retirement is to consider the following strategy:
1. Pay your taxes up front, and use the Roth 401(k) option instead of the Traditional 401(k) option; in this case, you are paying taxes on the "seed" and not on the "harvest"
2. Instead of contributing the maximum amount allowable into your Roth 401(k), contribute only up to the amount of your employer match; take the remaining funds that you would have contributed to the Roth 401(k) and invest them in a 7702 Plan account.
3. This approach will ensure that the vast majority of your retirement income will be tax free, only small percentage will be subjected to Market Volatility losses, and lastly, you will have a substantial death benefit to protect your family, both leading up to retirement as well as after retirement.

Time for a New Model

Over the last forty years we have watched the vast majority of employers eliminate employer sponsored pension plans, which would have paid the employee a guaranteed income for life after retirement, and replace them with 401(k) type plans, thus transferring both the burden and the cost of saving for retirement to the employee. Each employee is now responsible for funding and managing their own 401(k) type retirement savings account, with little or no training; further, the 401(k) plans have been subject to huge market losses during volatile market times, which have been both financially and emotionally devastating; on top of all of that, there is no guarantee of a stable income after retirement, and lastly, distributions from these plans are subject to unpredictable income taxes which can be increased at the whim of Congress.

In short, the 401(k) type savings plans have several major drawbacks and are failing us in a couple of critical areas; it's time, then, that we, the employees, take a new and closer look at the way we are approaching saving for our Retirement, making maximum use of vehicles such as financial planning, Roth IRAs, Roth 401(k)'s, and 7702 Account plans, among others.

And to that end, the recommended approach is to find and work with a true Financial Advisor, one who is a fiduciary*, and has the training, background, and licenses to take into account your entire retirement goals and needs, and structure the best possible plan for you utilizing all available programs and resources.

*The main responsibility of a fiduciary is to act solely in the interest of the client; this is a required status dictated by FINRA and the SEC for licensed Advisors; certain insurance agents without additional licenses do not have the training and are not held to the Fiduciary Standard.

Smart Retirement

Chapter 6: Social Security

Overview
The Social Security program is in place to provide a financial safety-net for working people and their families, when earnings come to a halt for a variety of reasons, including Retirement, Disability, or Death of the primary wage earner. Since the focus of this book is Retirement, the chapter will only focus on Social Security Retirement Benefits.

Please note: the source for all of the following material is: www.ssa.gov

Qualifying for Benefits
Originally, an individual qualified for Social Security Retirement benefits by working for ten years, earning 40 credits (one credit per quarter worked over the ten year period), and paying into the Social Security system. Recently, however, the way one earns credits has changed from quarters worked to a focus on income earned, again while paying into the system. In 2020, one credit is earned for each $1,410 earned during the year, up to a maximum of four credits per year. Once you have earned your 40 credits, the Social Security Administration calculates your benefits using a complex formula that encompasses total years worked and total amount contributed to the Social Security system.

What Will My Benefits Be?
The easiest way to find out a current estimate of your Social Security Retirement Benefits is to go online and set up an account at www.socialsecurity.gov, then click on "Estimate Your Retirement Benefits". Another approach is to use one of the calculators on the Social Security website: www.ssa.gov/planners/benefitcalculators.htm. Note that there has been an increase in Social Security Identity fraud, and regardless of the approach that you take, it is highly advisable that you at least sign up and establish your online account to prevent fraudsters from signing up in your name and potentially accessing your benefits.

Terms You Will Need to Know
You will see these terms mentioned throughout the Social Security website and paper statements:
- Primary Insurance Amount (PIA): this is the Social Security Retirement Benefit you will receive if you claim benefits at Full Retirement Age
- Full Retirement Age (FRA): this is the age at which a person is eligible to receive full Retirement Benefits; for those born before 1937, FRA is 65, and for those born later, FRA is between 65 and 2 months up to age 67, again depending on your year of birth (see table in the Appendix Section to determine your specific Full Retirement Age)

Starting Benefits Early

You can start taking your Social Security Retirement Benefits as early as age 62, regardless of your Full Retirement Age, but if you start before Full Retirement Age, your benefits will be reduced. Depending on your Full Retirement Age, your benefits will be reduced by between 25% and 30%. See table in the Appendix Section for reduction percentages for starting Social Security Benefits at any age prior to Full Retirement Age.

Benefits Can Increase by Waiting

Social Security allows you to receive Delayed Retirement Credits for every month that you postpone taking your Social Security Retirement Benefit after Full Retirement Age, up to attaining age 70. You will get an increase of about 8% for each year that you delay your benefits. See table in the Appendix Section for increased percentages for delaying Social Security Benefits.

Can You Continue to Work?

Of course you can continue to work after turning on your Social Security Retirement Benefits, however your benefit amount could be impacted depending upon both your age when your benefits start and the amount of money that you earn. The following describes this in more detail.

For those younger than full retirement age, you can earn up to a maximum of $18,240 in 2020 without being penalized; this amount is called the Social Security Earnings Cap or Earnings Limit; if you earn more than the Earnings Limit, however, you will lose $1 for every $2 earned above the Earnings Limit.

Beginning in the year that you attain full retirement age, but prior to the month that you reach full retirement age, you can earn a higher amount without losing benefits: in 2020 the Earnings Limit is $48,600, however, you will lose $1 for every $3 earned over that Earnings Limit. Starting in the month that you reach full retirement age, then, you can work and earn any amount without losing any of your benefits.

Taxes and Social Security

In 2020, if your Combined Income is above a certain amount, you will be required to pay taxes on you Social Security Retirement Benefits. The IRS defines Combined Income as your Adjusted Gross Income + Non-Taxable Interest Income + ½ of your Social Security Retirement Benefits (an around the block way for the government to tax supposed Federal Tax Free Municipal Bonds). If you are married and filing jointly:
    a. If your Combined Income is between $32,000 and $44,000, you will have to pay income tax on 50% of your Social Security Retirement Benefits
    b. If your Combined Income is more than $44,000, you will have to pay income tax on 85% of your Social Security Retirement Benefits

If you are single and filing as an individual:
   a. If your Combined Income is between $25,000 and $34,000, you will have to pay income tax on 50% of your Social Security Retirement Benefits
   b. If your Combined Income is more than $34,000, you will have to pay income tax on 85% of your Social Security Retirement Benefits

Please be aware that these limits and tax amounts are subject to change from year to year by the action of the U.S. Congress.

Spousal Benefits

There are different options available for Spouses depending upon whether they worked and paid into the Social Security system or not:

A Spouse who worked and is eligible for Social Security Retirement Benefits based on their own work record has the option to take benefits based on their own work record, or one-half of their Spouse's benefit, whichever is greater. Please keep in mind that to collect a Spousal Benefit, the other Spouse must have started collecting Social Security Retirement Benefits. Also note that Social Security Retirement benefits will be reduced if started prior to Full Retirement Age.

A Spouse who has not worked and/or has not paid into the Social Security system is considered a Nonqualifying Spouse; the Non Qualifying Spouse can still collect Social Security Retirement Benefits based on the record of a Qualifying Spouse, if they have been married for at least one year (or if married to the Spouse and is the parent of their child). If a Non Qualifying Spouse is at Full Retirement Age or later, they are eligible to receive 50% of the benefit amount of the Qualifying Spouse; however, if the Non-Qualifying Spouse is at least 62 years of age but not yet at Full Retirement Age, they will receive permanently reduced benefits. Once again, in order to receive Spousal Benefits, the Qualifying Spouse must have started collecting Social Security Retirement Benefits.

File-Restricted Strategy

To use this strategy, both Spouses must qualify for Social Security Retirement Benefits on their own, and both must have reached age 62 or older by 2015. To utilize this strategy, one Spouse must already be receiving Social Security Retirement Benefits; this then allows the other Spouse to start receiving a Spousal Benefit, while Delayed Retirement Credits are earned on their own benefits record. Delayed Retirement Credits are equal to an 8% per year increase in benefit amount until age 70, at which time the other Spouse can switch to receiving the Social Security Retirement Benefits based on their own higher amount.

Survivor Benefits

If you were married for at least 9 months prior to your Spouse's death, you will be eligible to receive Spousal Social Security Retirement Benefits beginning at your age 60 (or age 50 if you are disabled, or at any age if you have eligible children). Be aware, however, that if you begin receiving benefits prior to your Full Retirement Age, your benefits will be fractionally reduced.

Survivor Benefits are based on the Primary Insurance Amount of the deceased spouse on the date of death, including any Delayed Retirement Credits. Further, if you are eligible for benefits based on your own record, you can collect whichever benefit is higher, but you cannot collect both. Lastly, a surviving spouse who is eligible for their own benefits may collect survivor benefits while allowing the Delayed Retirement Credits to accrue on their own account, and then switch to their own account at a later time.

Final note: if you remarry before age 60 (or age 50 if disabled), you will not be eligible for Survivor Benefits unless that marriage ends. If you remarry after age 60, you will still be eligible to Survivor Benefits based on the work record of your deceased former spouse.

Benefits for a Divorced Spouse

As a divorced spouse, you may be eligible to receive Social Security Retirement Benefits (or even Survivor Benefits), under the following conditions:
   a. You must have been married for at least 10 years
   b. You must be at least age 62, although your benefits will be permanently reduced if started prior to your Full Retirement Age
   c. You must be currently unmarried; if you did remarry, and are currently divorced (or widowed), you will regain your eligibility
   d. The amount of your benefit will have no effect on your divorced spouse, or the benefit of any other ex-spouses.
   e. If you have been divorced for at least 2 years and you both are at least 62 years of age, you may get benefits even if your ex-spouse has not applied for theirs

Also be aware, that divorced spouses can are eligible to use the File Restricted strategy (as noted above) if they both turned 62 years old by 2015.

Special Pension Rules

There are special rules which will reduce your Social Security Retirement benefit if you have worked multiple jobs, receiving a government pension from one, and have paid into Social Security on the other. The federal government uses these rules to prevent full "double-dipping" of multiple pension sources. There are two different provisions: the Windfall Elimination Provision (WEP) and the Government Pension Offset (GPO), each described below.

Windfall Elimination Provision

The Windfall Elimination Provision (WEP) was enacted in 1983 and reduces Social Security benefit payments to beneficiaries whose work histories include both Social Security covered and non-Social Security covered employment (where Social Security taxes were not paid, and the non-covered employment also provides some form of pension coverage). In effect the WEP reduces eligible Social Security Retirement Benefits downward to prevent workers who will be receiving a government pension (from various government positions such as teachers, etc.) from also receiving Social Security Retirement Benefits as if they were long-time, low-wage-earning employees. A chart in the Appendix Section shows the maximum amount your Social Security Retirement Benefits may be reduced because of WEP.

Note: if you have worked at least 30 years or longer and have paid Social Security taxes throughout that time, WEP will not impact your Social Security Retirement Benefits.

Also Note: When WEP applies to a person's Social Security Benefit, it will also affect Spousal benefits, but does not affect Survivor benefits.

Government Pension Offset

The Government Pension Offset or GPO is a Social Security provision that penalizes individuals who receive Social Security Spousal or Survivor benefits, if they themselves worked for a state or local government in non-SS-covered employment and are entitled to a government pension from that employment. The GPO will reduce the Spousal or Survivor benefit by two-thirds of the amount of their non-Social Security covered pension; further, if their public pension receives a cost-of-living increase, their spousal or survivor benefit will be reduced by ⅔ of that amount as well.

Summary

As with other aspects of Retirement Planning, Social Security can be a complex and confusing topic, with options that, if not understood, could impact your retirement income for the rest of your life. As mentioned before, it is highly recommended that you find and work with a qualified and experienced Financial Advisor to help you understand and navigate the numerous options and complexities of Social Security.

Smart Retirement

Chapter 7
Healthcare Costs in Retirement

Longevity + Insufficient Savings = Inability to Pay for Health Care

Average Cost of Healthcare

Healthcare costs in retirement may be one of the biggest shocks that retirees will discover, as many people assume that upon turning 65, they will be receiving free Health Insurance, in the form of Medicare, for the rest of their lives. In reality, only the Medicare Part A premium is free (assuming you paid Medicare taxes while working). Medicare Part A, however, does have a deductible for hospital stays, while Medicare Part B (Outpatient Care and durable medical equipment) and Medicare Part D (Prescription Drug Plan) both have premiums, deductibles, and co-pays.

Cost of Medicare

Fidelity Investments publishes an annual survey of the total average estimated out of pocket cost for healthcare for a couple, both age 65, with the average life expectancies of 85 for a male and 87 for a female. For those turning 65 during 2019, the average estimated lifetime cost that this hypothetical couple will need is $285,000*. Generally, this figure will include:

- Medicare Premiums (Parts B and D)
- Medicare Deductibles
- Medicare Copays
- Medicare Supplemental Insurance (aka Medigap Insurance)
- Drug Copays and out of pocket expense for non-covered drugs
- Other over the counter medications and supplies

*Fidelity Notes and Disclaimer: The Healthcare Estimate is based on a hypothetical couple retiring in 2019, each 65-years-old, with average life expectancies of 85 for a male and 87 for a female. Estimates are calculated for "average" retirees, but may be more or less depending on actual health status, area of residence, and longevity. The Estimate assumes individuals do not have employer-provided retiree health care coverage, but do qualify for Original Medicare. The calculation takes into account cost-sharing provisions (such as deductibles and coinsurance) associated with Medicare Part A and Part B (inpatient and outpatient medical insurance). It also considers Medicare Part D (prescription drug coverage) premiums and out-of-pocket costs, as well as certain services excluded by Original Medicare. The estimate does not include other health-related expenses, such as over-the-counter medications, most dental services, vision, hearing, and long term care. Life expectancies based on research and analysis by Fidelity Investments Benefits Consulting group and data from the Society of Actuaries.

SOURCE: www.fidelity.com/about-fidelity/employer-services/health-care-costs-for-couples-in-retirement-rise

A Second Opinion

Another estimate is from HealthView Services (HVS), the nation's leading producer of Healthcare cost projection software and a thought leader producing educational content regarding healthcare costs; HVS projects that total out of pocket Healthcare costs for this same 65 year old couple in 2018 could be as high as $363,946. The following table details HVS's projections for couples turning 65, 55, and 45 in 2018:

	Premiums	Out-of-Pocket	Total Costs
65 Year Old Couple	$281,847	$82,099	$363.946
55 Year Old Couple	$300,548	$87,265	$387,814
45 Year Old Couple	$321,517	$93,299	$414,816

Source: www.hvsfinancial.com/2018-retirement-health-care-costs-data-report/

The HVS total out of pocket estimate includes expected vision, hearing, dental, other non-covered expenses, along with over the counter medications, supplies, and services.

Long Term Care Not Included

A potentially significant cost that is not included in either of the above estimates is the cost of Long Term Care and any associated Assisted Living expenses. Interestingly enough, Medicare does not consider Long Term Care as medical care, but rather, it is those custodial services required to meet a person's daily living needs. These custodial needs services are generally referred to as Activities of Daily Living and assistance with these needs would be similar to the care a parent would provide to a very young child. Long Term Care is further discussed in a subsequent Chapter.

Creating a Personal Estimate

As noted in the Introduction, the use of averages is useful in illustrating a broader point, yet individuals may want to create a customized estimate for themselves based on their own particular health, family history, and longevity factors. In that regard, the following tools can be useful in creating this personalized Healthcare estimation model:

Life Expectancy Calculator

Longevity is a key component when estimating total lifetime Healthcare costs in retirement; this first tool, then, is a life expectancy calculator found at: www.livingto100.com. According to the website, this tool "uses the most current and carefully researched medical and scientific data in order to estimate how old you will live to be"*. The calculator asks you 40 brief questions related to your health and family history, and takes about 10 minutes to complete. At the end, you will be asked to create an account to store your answers by providing your email address.

*Thomas Perls MD, MPH is the creator of the Life Expectancy Calculator and founder and director of the New England Centenarian Study, the largest study of centenarians and their families in the world. More can be learned about the study at **www.bumc.bu.edu/centenarian**.

Actuaries Longevity Illustrator

A second longevity tool is the Actuaries Longevity Illustrator, found at www.longevityillustrator.org. This tool, developed by the American Academy of Actuaries and the Society of Actuaries, is designed to provide "perspectives" on your longevity, including Planning Horizon probability graphs, arranged in order of percentage chances of living to various ages.

To use the Longevity Illustrator, you will need to answer a few questions about your health and your demographic characteristics. The Longevity Illustrator will then produce charts that allow you to see the probabilities associated with how long you (and your spouse/partner) might live (from your current age), which will help you understand the likelihood that you could live for a much longer or even a much shorter period of time than the general life expectancy charts might suggest.

AARP Healthcare Costs Calculator

The two longevity estimation tools above can assist you in estimating your own (and spouse/partner's) life expectancy; after coming up with your specific life expectancy, you are ready to create a personalized estimation of your Healthcare costs over your retirement lifespan. A very helpful tool for calculating this estimate is the AARP Personalized Healthcare Cost Estimator found at:
www.aarp.org/retirement/the-aarp-healthcare-costs-calculator/

This tool will have you enter your expected longevity number(s) calculated above, followed by entering some general information such as gender, age, height, weight, smoker, and state of residency. The tool will then provide a graph with total healthcare costs estimation based on demographics and expected age(s) provided. Results can be dramatically different than the averages provided initially, driven specifically by the individualized life expectancies and other demographic data provided. Additionally, the tool allows the creation of different potential outcomes by entering various health conditions found in your family history; you are encouraged to experiment with entering various health conditions to see how these conditions might affect your total estimated costs.

Final Calculation Note

There are many factors that affect longevity, including occupation, income, education level, gender, ethnicity, geography, smoking, weight, health, and family history; all of this information should be carefully considered when planning your income in retirement, and while no one wants to live shorter than their estimated life expectancy, there is a significant risk of running out of money if your retirement income is not carefully planned and monitored. Everyone is highly encouraged to seek qualified financial advice from an experienced Financial Advisor to ensure that they fully understand and plan for all significant cost risks relating to Healthcare throughout retirement.

Smart Retirement

Chapter 8: Understanding Medicare

Medicare Overview

A common misconception is that, upon turning 65 and signing up for Medicare, you will receive free healthcare for the rest of your life. Medicare as a whole (ie: with all of its Parts) is absolutely not free, and depending on the options selected, there will also be deductibles, co-pays, and limits to coverage. So, what exactly is Medicare? According to medicare.gov, Medicare is the federal health insurance program for people who are 65 or older; additionally, certain younger people with disabilities, and people with End-Stage Renal Disease (permanent kidney failure requiring dialysis or a transplant, sometimes called ESRD) are also eligible for Medicare. The Medicare program consists of several components, called Parts:

- Part A: Hospital Insurance
- Part B: Medical Insurance (doctors' services, outpatient care, medical supplies, and preventive services)
- Part C: Medicare Advantage Plans (Plans offered by private companies that provide hospitalization, outpatient treatment, and doctor visits that replace Part A and Part B)
- Part D: Prescription Drug coverage
- Medicare Supplemental Insurance (sometimes called Medigap Insurance), covers some of the "gaps" in Medicare Health Insurance coverage, such as deductibles and co-pays.

Medicare Part A

Medicare Part A, also known as Original Medicare, covers inpatient care in a hospital. It also covers skilled nursing care, hospice, and home health care if you meet certain conditions. Medicare Part A **does not** cover Assisted Living or non-skilled nursing care costs. Assisted Living or other Home Health Care, also known as Long Term Care, is not considered medical care, but rather assistance with the basic personal tasks of everyday life.

Most people will not have to pay a Part A premium because they paid Medicare taxes while working, however, without additional or supplemental coverage, there is both an initial deductible and a daily deductible for all hospital admissions, which can be substantial and generally change (rise) annually. If you are already receiving Social Security benefits, you will automatically be enrolled starting the first day of the month that you turn 65; if you are not receiving Social Security, you will need to contact Social Security three months prior to turning 65 years of age in order to sign up for benefits.

Medicare Part B

Medicare Part B generally covers medically necessary services like doctor visits, outpatient care, home health service, durable medical equipment, and various other medical services. Most people will pay the standard monthly premium, although premiums are higher for people with moderately higher incomes. As with Medicare

Part A, unless you have additional or supplemental coverage, you will pay an annual deductible and a co-pay for each service, currently set at 20% of the Medicare approved amount for the service. Also, like Medicare Part A, if you are already receiving Social Security benefits, you will automatically be enrolled starting the first day of the month that you turn 65; if you are not receiving Social Security, you will need to contact Social Security three months prior to turning 65 years of age. Also note that if you are receiving Social Security Benefits, your Medicare Part B Premium will be automatically deducted from your monthly benefit payment.

Medicare Part C – Medicare Advantage Plans
A Medicare Advantage Plan is a type of Medicare health plan offered by a private company that contracts with Medicare to provide you with all of your Part A and Part B benefits. Medicare Advantage Plans generally include Health Maintenance Organizations (HMOs), Preferred Provider Organizations (PPOs), Private Fee-for-Service Plans, Special Needs Plans, and Medicare Medical Savings Account Plans. If you're enrolled in a Medicare Advantage Plan, Medicare services are covered and paid for through the plan and are not paid for by Medicare.

Medicare Advantage Plans will generally have higher monthly premiums than government sponsored Part A and Part B Plans, and premiums are dependent on the types of plan and types of services that you select. Most Medicare Advantage Plans also offer prescription drug coverage for an additional monthly premium.

Medicare Part D – Prescription Drug Plans
Medicare Prescription Drug Plans (sometimes called "PDPs") add prescription drug coverage to Original Medicare, and are offered through private insurance providers, for an additional monthly premium. Part D plans are not required to pay for all drugs, but instead, each plan establishes a list of drugs that they will cover, and organizes the covered drugs into tiers; each tier is associated with a set co-pay amount, and the lower the tier, the lower the co-pay amount. Note that if you are receiving Social Security Benefits, your Medicare Part D Premium will be automatically deducted from your monthly benefit payment.

Finally, be aware that if you do not enroll when first eligible, and decide to join later, you will be assessed a late enrollment penalty.

Note: The average nationwide monthly premium for Part D Drug Plans for 2020 is $47.59, however Plan costs vary based on the plan you choose and where you live, and is further defined below.

Medicare Part D Premiums
Medicare Part D premiums depend on the plan chosen and where you live. Some thought needs to go into your choice of plan because each plan dictates the annual deductible, the copay amount, and the coinsurance amount. Obviously, the lower the deductible, the higher the premium will be; similarly, copay and coinsurance amounts are based on the type of drugs covered, from generic to specialty, and are grouped into four different Tiers. The table below outlines the four Tiers:

Part D Copay Tiers

Tier 1: Generic	Tier 2: Preferred	Tier 3: Non-Preferred	Tier 4: Specialty
$	$$	$$$	$$$$
All generic drugs and select brand names	Brand name drugs that have proven to be most effective in their class	Brand name drugs that have not been proven to be the most effective plus Preferred Specialty drugs	Brand name specialty and not preferred drugs

Source: www.mymedicarematters.org/costs/part-d/

Coverage Gap

Medicare Part D has an initial coverage limit, up to a point where catastrophic coverage begins; this coverage gap is informally known as the donut hole. For 2018, the initial coverage limit is $3,750; after reaching this limit, you will then be responsible for paying all drug costs up to $5,000, and after paying this amount, catastrophic coverage will begin. In the catastrophic coverage phase, Medicare will pay the majority of all the drug costs, but you will still be liable for a copay or coinsurance amount, again, depending on your plan and the type of drugs needed. Note that copays and coinsurance payments up to the point of entering the gap are not counted toward the payments required while in the gap.

Source: www.mymedicarematters.org/costs/part-d/

Medicare Supplement (Medigap) Plans

A Medicare Supplement or Medigap plan is additional insurance sold by private companies. As the name implies, these plans can pay for some or all of the health care costs that Original Medicare doesn't cover, like copayments, coinsurance, and deductibles. Additionally, some Medigap policies offer coverage for services that Original Medicare doesn't cover, like medical care when you travel outside the U.S. A Medigap policy is different from a Medicare Advantage Plan in that the Advantage Plans are ways to get Medicare benefits through a private insurer, while a Medigap policy supplements your Original Medicare benefits, and can pay a portion or all of your deductibles and your co-pays. There are currently ten standardized Medicare Supplement plans, designated by the letters A through N; each letter represents a coverage plan with benefits stipulated by the federal government. Premiums for the Supplemental Plans vary by both the Insurance carrier and the plan itself, however the benefits for each individual lettered plan will be the same, regardless of the provider. Overall, Supplemental Plans tend to be the best option (ie: better than a Medicare Advantage Plan) if you can afford the monthly premiums.

Some additional notes about Supplemental Plans are:

- Medigap / Supplemental Plans are pure insurance products, and generally function the same as private health insurance products with regard to pre-existing conditions
- An exception to the preexisting condition rule is that most plans are guaranteed issue if you purchase the plan when you enroll in Medicare Parts A and B; changing providers at a later date, with a preexisting condition, may not be possible, or may result in a drastic premium increase
- All Medigap plans are guaranteed renewable, even if you develop serious health issues
- Currently, Medigap policies do not cover Prescription Drugs; you will still need to enroll in Medicare Part D for Prescription Drug coverage

One final note: Medigap policies generally do not cover long-term care, glasses and vision care, dental care, hearing aids, or private-duty nursing.
Source for all Medicare and Medigap information: www.medicare.gov

Means Testing
Medicare currently provides health coverage to over 50 million subscribers, and further, as approximately 10,000 baby boomers turn 65 each day, Medicare enrollment is estimated to reach 64 million by 2020 and 81 million by 2030*. This, coupled with a projection of only 2.5 workers to every retiree by 2030, has forced Congress to implement "Means Testing" to assist in keeping the Medicare program solvent. What this means is that those with higher incomes in retirement will pay more for continued enrollment in the program.

Means Testing is implemented by levying surcharges based on your Modified Adjusted Gross Income (MAGI). The table in the Appendix Section details the current surcharges associated with each MAGI level.

*Source: http://www.ncpssm.org/Medicare/MedicareFastFacts

Sources for above and for additional information Securing Today and Tomorrow 2018 edition:
www.ssa.gov/pubs/EN-05-10536.pdf

www.medicare.gov/part-d/costs/premiums/drug-plan-premiums.html

Understanding MAGI
The federal government takes the broadest approach for calculating your Modified Adjusted Gross Income (MAGI) and the associated Medicare surcharges, by including almost every possible source of income, including: Social Security, pensions, wages (when working in retirement), earned interest, and capital gains from investment income. Additionally, they also include income from tax-free Municipal Bonds and Required Minimum Distributions from IRA accounts. Finally, there is a two year "look-back" period when calculating current year MAGI and Medicare surcharges, meaning that your 2020 Medicare premiums would be based on your 2018 Modified Adjusted Gross Income..

Based on the above, then, it is clear that a middle-class individual with a pension and a few investments (even investments in so-called tax-free Municipal Bonds) is considered affluent according to Medicare; this would mean that the individual could end up in the second or third tier income bracket, facing substantial additional Medicare expenses, expenses that most have probably failed to factor into their retirement budgets.

Options to Consider
Various products such as Roth IRAs and Roth 401ks, Health Savings Accounts (HSAs), certain types of Life Insurance, non-qualified annuities, and even Reverse Mortgages can be utilized to effectively lower your MAGI. For more information about various strategies for lowering MAGI please seek the advice and assistance from a qualified and experienced Financial Advisor, Tax Accountant, or Tax Attorney.

In Summary
As you can see, understanding the terminology and various coverage plans in the Medicare program can be confusing and quite difficult; further, some decisions that need to be made upon initial enrollment could remain in place for the rest of your life; and finally, income strategies and MAGI need to be understood to avoid costly surprises. For all of these reasons it is highly recommended that people approaching the age of 65 seek the advice of a qualified Financial Advisor, Insurance Agent, Tax Accountant, or Tax Attorney prior to making any final decisions on any of the Medicare options.

Contacting Medicare
For additional information on Medicare, the U.S. Government publishes a comprehensive and informative book each year entitled "***Medicare & You***". It is the official government handbook and is available **free** of charge in either paper form or in an electronic document in pdf format. You can order your free copy by visiting: **www.medicare.gov/publications**

The publication is updated annually and remember, this information is provided **free of charge**; be aware of what you are purchasing if someone wants to charge you for information alone.

Smart Retirement

Contacting Medicare

To obtain personalized Help over the phone, call toll-free, **1-800-MEDICARE (1-800-633-4227)** (for the deaf or hard of hearing, call the TTY number, **1-800-486-2048**). Information is available 24 hours a day, 7 days a week. Additionally, a wealth of Medicare information is available online at:

www.medicare.gov

State Health Insurance Assistance Program (SHIP)

What is SHIP?

SHIP is a free health benefits counseling service for Medicare beneficiaries and their families or caregivers. SHIP's mission is to educate, advocate, counsel and empower people to make informed healthcare benefit decisions. SHIP is an independent program funded by Federal agencies and is not affiliated with the insurance industry.

SHIP Counseling is FREE of charge

State Health Insurance Assistance Programs (SHIPs) provide free help to Medicare beneficiaries who have questions or issues with their health insurance. You can call a counselor or attend a workshop/presentation in your area.

Each state has their own SHIP program; the following website provides overview and contact information for each state:

www.seniorsresourceguide.com/directories/National/SHIP/

Direct Primary Care

One of the biggest issues facing anyone retiring before becoming eligible for Medicare at age 65 is finding affordable Health Insurance coverage; this is where Direct Primary Care might be the answer. Direct Primary Care, or DPC is an innovative payment model where patients have extraordinary access to their Primary Care Physician for a simple fee generally less than $100 per month, with additional discounts for adding a spouse and/or children. For additional information, or to find a Direct Primary Physician in your area, simply google: Direct Primary Care.

Chapter 9: Understanding Medicaid

Medicaid Overview
Although some people confuse the two, Medicare and Medicaid are completely separate programs. Medicare (generally speaking) provides health insurance coverage for those 65 and older, with premium costs (again generally speaking) paid out of pocket or directly from one's Social Security Retirement Income. Medicaid, on the other hand, provides health coverage for very low-income people, families and children, pregnant women, the elderly, and people with disabilities; generally speaking, these are people living at or below the federally defined poverty level, and Medicaid services will be provided free of charge.

Although Medicaid programs must follow federal guidelines, they are administered by, and vary somewhat, from state to state. It is generally considered to be the healthcare provider of last resort for those living at or below the poverty level.

Medicaid and Long Term Care
Medicaid is typically the safety net for long-term care services for those living below the poverty level or who become impoverished as a result of disabling illness or injury. Individuals who apply for Medicaid assistance with assisted living or nursing home care are subject to a "look back" period of five years for asset transfers, during which eligibility may be denied or penalties imposed. This "look back" is intended to prevent those above the eligibility levels for Medicaid from giving away their assets in order to qualify for Medicaid. On the other hand, however, unplanned catastrophic health issues or sudden and unexpected Long Term Care costs could quickly place a family in severe financial difficulty. For those who feel that potential or looming healthcare costs could bankrupt and impoverish the family, leaving them destitute, certain legal strategies are available if pursued well in advance. Certain of these strategies are discussed in the following chapters, however, any of these strategies will require the assistance and guidance from a qualified Estate Planning or Eldercare Attorney. If you think this may become an issue for you, you are encouraged to get the facts from a qualified attorney sooner than later.

Contacting Medicaid
Medicaid is a state administered program and each state sets its own guidelines regarding eligibility and services. For additional information on Medicaid, visit:
www.medicaid.gov

Smart Retirement

Chapter 10: Long Term Care

Long Term Care Defined
According to the U.S. Department of Health and Human Services, Administration on Aging (AOA), Long Term Care is defined as a range of services and supports that are required by people with a chronic illness or a serious disability. More specifically, that Long Term Care does not mean medical care, but rather, those custodial services required to meet a person's daily living needs. These custodial needs services are generally referred to as Activities of Daily Living and assistance with these needs would be similar to the care a parent would provide to a very young child. The six general Activities of Daily Living would include:
- Transferring from bed to chair or vice versa
- Dressing
- Bathing
- Eating
- Getting to and from the toilet
- Caring for incontinence

Additionally, other common Long Term Care service requirements may include:
- Preparing food and cleaning up after meals
- Housework and general house cleaning
- Managing money and paying bills
- Taking medication
- Shopping for groceries or clothes
- Caring for pets
- Responding to emergency alerts such as fire alarms

When thinking of Long Term Care, then, Assisted Living or Nursing Homes may come to mind, yet these services can be offered in a person's own home or even in an adult day-care setting. In any event, around the clock assistance for chronically ill people can become very expensive and quickly deplete a person's remaining financial resources.

Source: http://longtermcare.gov/the-basics/ (As of 3-19-2015)

Who Needs Long Term Care?
The duration and extent of a person's Long Term Care needs will obviously depend on a number of factors, such as the type of illness or injury, and will generally change over time as that person ages. Consider the following statistics from the Administration on Aging:
- An estimated 70% of all people turning 65 will require some form of Long Term Care during their lifetime, and 20% will need it for more than 5 years
- The older you are, the more likely you will need Long Term Care

- Men generally need Long Term Care an average of 2.2 years
- Since women outlive men by an average of five years, they will generally need Long Term Care longer: an average of 3.7 years
- An estimated 69% of people age 90 or older currently have a disability and require Long Term Care
- Chronic conditions such as diabetes and high blood pressure make you more likely to need care; your family history such as whether your parents or grandparents had chronic conditions, may also increase the likelihood of needing Long Term Care.
- Poor diet and poor exercise habits increase your chances of needing Long Term Care.

Source: http://longtermcare.gov/the-basics/ (As of 3-19-2015)

Who Pays for Long Term Care?

There seems to be a common yet colossal misconception that Social Security and/or Medicare will pay the cost of Long Term Care, but this is absolutely false. To be more specific, unless you have Long Term Care Insurance, you or your family will generally have to pay for Long Term Care services, and further, will have to pay for services that are not covered by the Long Term Care policy. Some facts:

Medicare

Medicare only pays for services in a Nursing Home or Skilled Services setting, and only for a maximum of 100 days. Skilled Service is generally defined as trained medical professionals, such as nurses or rehabilitation therapy-providers.

Medicare, then, **does not pay** for Non-Skilled assistance with Activities of Daily Living (ie: those activities outlined above), in settings such as Assisted Living facilities or in the person's own home, which comprise the vast majority of Long-Term Care needs.

Medicaid

Medicaid may pay for Long Term Care services, but to qualify, your income and personal assets must be below a certain, very low level, which generally means at or below the poverty level.

Other Federal Government Programs:

Other federal programs, such as those established under the Older Americans Act and programs for veterans provided by the Department of Veterans Affairs, **may** pay for some Long Term Care services, however, only for specific populations and only in certain circumstances (ie: generally low income people living at or below the poverty level).

Health Insurance Plans:

Like Medicare, most employer-sponsored Health Insurance plans and virtually all private Health Insurance plans cover only Skilled Services, or services in a Nursing

Home or Skilled Services setting, and **do not cover** non-Skilled assistance with Activities of Daily Living, regardless of the setting.

Private Long Term Care Insurance:
As mentioned above, a private Long Term Care Insurance plan is generally the only insurance coverage available to pay for Long Term Care services (ie: assistance with Activities of Daily Living); typically, these private Long Term Care policies will pay a fixed daily rate for services provided in either a private home or in an Assisted Living facility. Additional information on Private Long Term Care Insurance is provided below.

> ### Older Americans Act
> The Older Americans Act (OAA), originally enacted in 1965, supports a range of home and community-based services, such as meals-on-wheels and other nutrition programs, in-home services, transportation, legal services, elder abuse prevention and caregivers support. These programs were designed to help seniors stay as independent as possible in their homes and communities, avoiding more costly hospitalization and Nursing Home care, thus saving federal and state funds that otherwise would be spent on such care. Currently, low funding levels for the OAA leave many needs unmet, increasing reliance on more expensive medical and institutional care.
>
> Source: http://www.aoa.gov/AOA_programs/OAA/index.aspx (As of 3-19-2015)

Benefits for Veterans
Veterans and survivors who are eligible for a VA pension and require the aid and attendance of another person, either in their own home or in an assisted living or nursing home facility, may be eligible for additional financial assistance under either the Aid and Attendance program or the Housebound program. These are benefits that would be paid in addition to the VA monthly pension.

Aid and Attendance
For a wartime Veteran or surviving Spouse to qualify for an Aid and Attendance monthly pension, the Veteran must have served at least 90 days of active military service, at least one day of which was during a period of war, and be discharged under conditions other than dishonorable. Wartime Veterans who entered active duty on or after September 7, 1980, must have completed at least 24 continuous months of military service or the period for which they were ordered to active duty.

Aid and Attendance is a "needs based" program; to qualify financially, an applicant must have on average less than $80,000 in assets, excluding their home and vehicles. If qualified, the Aid and Attendance program currently provides the veteran up to $700 per month to cover the cost of assistance with Activities of Daily Living.

Since Aid and Attendance and Housebound allowances increase the pension amount, people who are not eligible for a basic pension due to excessive income may be eligible for pension at these increased rates. Aid and Attendance benefits can provide up to $700 per month in addition to a veteran's VA pension benefits, and about $500 per month extra to a survivor's VA Death Pension.

Although Aid and Attendance is a needs-based program, certain Trust vehicles may be able to assist a wartime veteran with assets exceeding the maximum to qualify for this program. For further information on your own specific circumstances, you will need to seek the advice and counsel of a qualified Eldercare attorney.

Housebound Benefits
A veteran who is receiving a VA pension, or a survivor receiving a VA Death Pension, may also be eligible for Housebound benefits if one or more of these conditions apply to the veteran or survivor:
- They have a single, permanent, 100% disability, and, due to that disability, are permanently and substantially confined to their home; or
- They have a single, permanent, 100% disability and also have another disability or disabilities evaluated as 60 percent or more disabling.

Housebound benefits can provide up to $200 a month to a veteran's pension benefits, and up to about $150 per month extra to a survivor's VA Death Pension. A Veteran or surviving spouse may not receive Aid and Attendance benefits and Housebound benefits at the same time.

Source and for additional information:
www.benefits.va.gov/pension/aid_attendance_housebound.asp

Veterans Administration

For more information and to find copies of various forms and other related publications, visit the Veterans Administration website at **www.va.gov** or call toll-free, **1-800-827-1000** (for the deaf or hard of hearing, call the TTY number, **1-800-829-4833**). Telephone hours of operation vary from department to department, but, all are only available Monday through Friday. Certain questions can be answered by the automated system which is available 24 hours a day, 7 days a week.

Military Records
In order to begin the application process for any Veterans benefits, you will need to have a copy of the Veterans form DD-214 (Report of Separation). If you are unable to locate this form, any member of the immediate family can request a free copy from the U.S. Government National Archive Office in St. Louis, by going online to:

www.archives.gov/veterans/military-service-records/

Private Long Term Care Insurance

Unlike traditional Health Insurance plans, Long Term Care Insurance is designed to cover the cost of providing custodial care for those needing assistance with Activities of Daily Living. The cost of custodial care is typically computed on a cost-per-day basis, and Long Term Care policies generally reimburse the policyholder a daily, pre-set amount. This allows you to choose to be cared for in your home or in an Assisted Living facility, and also to choose only those services which you need and can afford.

Purchasing Long Term Care Insurance

The cost of Long Term Care policies varies not only between the different companies that offer them, but also on a number of other factors including:

- **Benefit amount and duration**: Rates will be higher for policies with higher benefit amounts and longer payment durations. Benefit periods are generally one, two, three, or five years, or for a lifetime.
- **Elimination period**: Rates will be higher for policies with benefits beginning sooner; the longer a person can afford to pay their own expenses before the policy begins paying benefits, the lower premiums will be.
- **Age**: The younger an applicant is, the lower the premium will be; statistically, the insurance company will receive more premiums prior to paying out any benefits.
- **Health**: A person's health at the time the policy is applied for will affect the premium; obviously the premium will be higher if the insurance company believes that it will begin paying benefits ahead of others in the same age bracket. Be aware that some people in poor health may not qualify at all.
- **Other factors**: Various other factors and policy provisions will also affect the premium:
    - Long Term Care costs vary greatly from one area of the country to another.
    - The maximum number of days, months, or years that the policy will pay is optional and will cost more for a longer payout period.
    - Inclusion of an inflation rider, where benefit payments can increase with the cost of living, will also cost more than a policy with a fixed, level benefit payment. And remember that while a benefit of $150 a day may appear adequate in today's dollars, it could turn out to be woefully inadequate 20 or 30 years in the future.

One additional note: while policies are generally guaranteed renewable, once purchased, the premiums will generally rise over time; it is important to at least review a company's rate increase history prior to purchasing a Long Term Care policy.

Hybrid Life Insurance Products

Some people are reluctant to purchase Long Term Care insurance with the thought that, like owning automobile insurance and never having an accident, the invested money will be lost if it is never used.

Some Life Insurance Companies today, however, have attempted to solve this problem by combining life insurance with Long Term Care riders, that will pay a stipulated amount toward Long Term Care should that need arise, or pay a death benefit to the heirs should Long Term Care never be needed. It is interesting to note that, like a Life Insurance Death Benefit payment, Long Term Care benefit payments are generally federal tax free.

These types of products are relatively new and features are continuing to change as the product evolves. For additional information on any of these types of products, you will need to consult with a qualified Financial Advisor or Insurance Agent.

Annuities

As noted above, proceeds from Long Term Care policies are generally received tax free. All gains within a deferred annuity, however, are subject to ordinary income tax when withdrawn. Under the Pension Protection Act of 2006, however, withdrawals from certain deferred annuity policies can be taken tax free if used to purchase a Long Term Care policy, through a 1035 exchange. This basically has the effect of allowing the purchase of Long Term Care policies with tax free dollars, and, subject to certain limits, assures that the money will never be taxed when later received in the form of a benefit payout from the Long Term Care policy.

Note: Using annuity value may reduce your ability to produce income or reduce the amount available to heirs for income or savings. You may also never use the full benefit under a Long Term Care contract for which you paid. Other federal or state tax deductions may be available that may be more advantageous.

If you own a deferred annuity, or are considering purchasing one, you might want to get more information on this approach by speaking with a qualified Financial Advisor.

Other Options

At this point, we should all understand that the cost of Long Term Care can get to be exorbitantly expensive and can rapidly exhaust a family's life savings, even if there is a Long Term Care policy in place. Should a family find itself in that position, there are a few other options that can be considered to assist with the financial burden:

Reverse Mortgage

A reverse mortgage is a special type of loan, available to homeowners who are 62 years or older, that enables them to convert a portion of the equity in their home into cash. Obviously this option would only be of benefit to those who actually had a substantial amount of equity in their home, and further, there are a number of potential draw-backs:

- Fees will impact the amount of cash that you will receive
- The homeowner is still responsible for upkeep and all maintenance of the house
- Generally higher interest rate than traditional home equity loans

- Typically, the house will be sold upon your death leaving little or nothing to your heirs
- You would have to repay the loan should you move out; typically, this is defined as not living in the home for one year, and there are no exceptions should you have to be in an Assisted Living facility for this period of time

Despite the potential draw-backs, this may be one of the only solutions available for a person facing increasing Long Term Care expenses, and could additionally free up funds that the family would otherwise have to pay to meet the monthly mortgage expense.

Note: Reverse Mortgages are highly complex. You should consult a qualified tax professional, attorney, or reverse mortgage counselor to discuss your options. You can also visit the National Council on Aging at www.ncoa.org for more information on reverse mortgages.

Life Insurance Options
If you own certain types of Life Insurance, the policy may provide for ways to receive the death benefit prior to your death. Three possible options are explained below:

Accelerated Death Benefits
An Accelerated Death Benefit feature is included in some life insurance policies that will allow a person to receive a tax-free advance on their life insurance death benefit while still alive. This feature is generally only available with permanent type life insurance, although there are some instances where it is available with term life insurance. Normally, there would be an extra charge to have this feature added to a policy. Generally, the Accelerated Death Benefit would be available if:
- You have a terminal illness
- You have a life-threatening diagnosis, such as AIDS
- You need long-term care services for an extended amount of time
- You are permanently confined to a nursing home and incapable of performing Activities of Daily Living (ADL), such as dressing, eating, or bathing

The amount of benefit received from an Accelerated Death Benefit can vary by policy and company, but it is generally capped at 50 percent of the policy's death benefit. This is not true in all instances, as some policies will allow payment of the full amount of the death benefit. Once again, this depends on both the policy itself and the issuing company. Any payments from an Accelerated Death Benefit are of course subtracted from the final death benefit to be paid out.

For Accelerated Death Benefit policies that cover Long Term Care services, the benefit is usually a monthly payment; Nursing Home care might typically receive two percent of the life insurance policy's face value, while the amount available for home care is typically half that amount. The total benefit payout, however, would still be subject to the overall payout cap.

One final note: depending on the policy amount, there may be little or no health screenings required. Should you have a health condition that might exclude you from Long Term Care eligibility, you might still consider a Life Insurance policy with an Accelerated Death Benefit feature.

Viatical Settlements*

A Viatical Settlement is completely different from an Accelerated Death Benefit, and occurs when a third party actually purchases the life insurance policy death benefit for a lump sum of cash, generally more than the cash-surrender value but only a percentage of the stated death benefit. The amount of the settlement is typically dependent on the person's life expectancy, and could range from as high as 80% for a person with less than 6 months to live to perhaps 50% for a person with more than two years to live. The third party becomes the new owner of the policy, continues to pay the premiums, and receives the full death benefit when the person dies.

Some key points to consider when contemplating a Viatical Settlement:

- A Viatical Settlement can only be used if you are terminally ill and have a life expectancy of two years or less
- Viatical companies are very particular and do not approve all applicants
- Money received from a Viatical Settlement is generally received tax free
- If you sell your policy to a Viatical company, your heirs will no longer receive the death benefit

Life Settlements*

Viatical Settlements became popular during the 1980s as a way for AIDS patients and other terminally ill policyholders to obtain some cash from their life insurance policy before they died. As stated above, Viatical Settlements are arranged only for people with life expectancies of fewer than two years. Life Settlements, on the other hand, generally cover people age 65 and older who are not terminally ill but have life expectancies of between two and 10 years. For seniors in this category, a life settlement will generally yield a much higher payout than the policy's current cash value for those no longer able or wanting to continue to pay the premiums.

Some key points to consider when contemplating a Life Settlement:
- The process generally does not require any **health screening**; you may be in good or poor health
- A portion of the proceeds of the sale may be **taxed**
- If you sell your policy for a Life Settlement, your heirs will no longer receive the death benefit

*****Note**: Viatical and Life Settlements are highly complex products and companies marketing them must be licensed by the state in which they operate. Additionally, there has been numerous cases of fraud surrounding these types of products, so you will need to consult a qualified tax professional, attorney, or financial advisor to discuss and understand your options prior to proceeding.

Source: U.S. Department of Health and Human Services (LongTermCare.gov):
http://longtermcare.gov/costs-how-to-pay/paying-privately/annuities/ (As of 3-19-2015)

Special Considerations for Alzheimer's and Dementia

While people with dementia can remain in their own home for some length of time, eventually they will need professional help and constant supervision. And further, once symptoms of dementia begin to appear, the Long Term Care planning process can become much more complex if the Advance Directives (as outlined in the Chapter Section entitled: Advance Directives) are out of date or have never been completed.:

- The inability to comprehend finances and care choices is often among the first signs of dementia
- Advanced Care Directive needs to be in place and current to ensure medical treatment choices reflect the person's preferences, and not the guess of the caregiver
- Medical Power of Attorney also needs to be in place and current to ensure that the right person (or persons) are in place to make medical treatment decisions for those no longer able to communicate their wishes
- Durable Power of Attorney for Finances needs to be in place and current to ensure financial decisions can be made to pay for care, apply for assistance, and for all other ongoing payment requirements

Additional in-depth information on Alzheimer's Disease can be found at the U.S. government official website:
http://alzheimers.gov/

And also at the Alzheimer's Association official website:
http://alz.org/

Special Assistance for Texas Residents:

The Texas Long-Term Care Partnership was created by the Texas Legislature to give Texans information and tools needed to plan for long-term care. The Partnership is a collaborative effort between private long-term care insurance providers, their authorized agents, and state government agencies, including the Texas Department of Insurance, the Texas Health and Human Services Commission, and the Texas Department of Aging and Disability Services. More information is available at:
www.ownyourfuturetexas.org/about

Additionally, the site provides a ten question self-assessment tool for determining your risk of needing Long Term Care:
www.ownyourfuturetexas.org/long-term-care-assessment

Residents of other states should check with their own state's office of aging for similar programs and/or additional information.

Assisted Living

Long Term Care can be administered within a person's own home, or, if the situation is severe enough, a person will actually need to move into an Assisted Living facility, where round the clock assistance is available for custodial care, or all tasks associated with the Activities of Daily Living.

Not a Nursing Home

An Assisted Living facility is not a Nursing Home, although the terms are sometimes mistakenly used interchangeably. To differentiate, a Nursing Home is a facility designed to provide the highest level of **medical care** for elderly patients outside of a hospital. Although Nursing Homes may provide some level of **custodial care**, it is secondary to their role of providing medical care; a licensed physician is always assigned to supervise each patient's care and a nurse or other high level medical professional is always on the premises.

The name "Nursing Home" generally has a negative connotation, likely because of the institutional approach that they employ and the fact that very sick or extremely disabled people are cared for in those facilities; generally speaking, however, Nursing Home patients may never recover or may stabilize to the point where they can take care of themselves and leave the Nursing Home.

An Assisted Living facility, on the other hand, is a senior living option for those with minimal medical requirements, but needing assistance with some or even all of the Activities of Daily Living (this type of assistance is also referred to as custodial care). The major focus of Assisted Living arrangements, then, is helping older adults live as independently as possible, while providing assistance as needed for Activities of Daily Living. Once again, some common examples of Activities of Daily Living include some or all of the following:

- Transferring from bed to chair or vice versa
- Dressing
- Bathing
- Eating
- Using the toilet (and caring for incontinence)

Additionally, other common custodial Long Term Care service requirements may also include:
- Preparing food and cleaning up after meals
- Housework and general house cleaning
- Managing money and paying bills
- Taking medication
- Shopping for groceries or clothes

- Caring for pets
- Responding to emergency alerts such as fire alarms

But once again, these are not medical requirements, they are custodial in nature; the overriding goal of Assisted Living, then, is to emphasize choice, dignity, privacy, and independence; indeed, the best Assisted Living facilities aim to provide their residents with the privacy and comforts of home, while providing a sense of safety and security by offering the required assistance for Activities of Daily Living.

Do the Research First
The goal of all businesses is to generate a return on their investment for the owners, yet there is a significant difference between how profits are allocated in for-profit and not-for-profit organizations. The objective of a for-profit company is to make a profit and distribute those gains to the owners or shareholders, while a non-profit entity must use its funds solely for the mission for which it was formed. This is not to say that a not-for-profit facility is generally better than a for-profit facility; it merely means that, as always, it pays to do all of your research in advance prior to selecting a facility for yourself or a loved one.

Tips to Consider
While Nursing Homes are highly regulated, and the ratings of all Nursing Homes are available on the medicare.gov website, the opposite is unfortunately true for Assisted Living facilities: there are currently no federal laws and very few state laws regulating the Assisted Living industry. It is extremely important, then, that consumers thoroughly research their selection prior to making a commitment for themselves or a loved one to any Assisted Living facility.

Some general tips to consider when selecting an Assisted Living facility would include the following:
1. Look for reviews of the candidate facility online, through the Better Business Bureau, and your state's office on the elderly and aging
2. Get feedback from current residents and their families
3. Determine for yourself if the level of staff to resident ratio is adequate
4. Understand the overnight procedures and determine for yourself if the number of staff on duty overnight is adequate
5. Get a feel for the comfort and versatility of the resident rooms
6. Examine the community spaces for comfort and determine conduciveness to support the disabled in general, and your care needs in particular
7. Pay special attention to overall cleanliness; in particular, the smell of urine should be a definite red flag of concern
8. Visit the facility during activities periods and eat a meal with the residents
9. Pay particular attention to the attitudes and friendliness of the staff
10. Understand the contract and ask detail questions prior to signing
11. Understand your "move-out" options, and likewise, understand the circumstances required for eviction
12. Visit several facilities and comparison shop: facilities, staffing, activities, pricing

13. Do not make price the most important criteria, as you will generally get what you pay for
14. Listen to your instincts: they are generally correct.

Assisted Living: Final Thoughts
The general concept of Assisted Living, a safe and comfortable living arrangement, with dedicated, on-site assistance for Activities of Daily Living, in a community of other seniors, has a great deal of appeal for families struggling with the issues of how best to care for an aging loved one, especially a loved one in cognitive decline. On the other hand, the loss of independence, dignity, and personal privacy can have a devastating effect on the very loved one we are hoping to protect, and the institutionalized approach utilized by a large number of Assisted Living facilities can tend to exacerbate the three plagues of the elderly: boredom, loneliness, and helplessness. It's a balancing act, then, with cost and convenience on one hand, and the life of an elderly loved one on the other; the only recommendation: do the research, choose wisely, and watch closely.

Exploring Life Beyond Adulthood:
The Eden Alternative
The Green House Project

Dr. Bill Thomas is an international expert on elderhood and geriatric medicine. He is the founder of the Eden Alternative and the Green House Project, and the author of "What Are Old People For" and "Second Wind". The Eden Alternative is an international, non-profit organization dedicated to creating quality of life for Elders and their care partners, wherever they may live.
www.edenalt.org/about-the-eden-alternative

The Green House Project is a unique approach to Assisted Living designed to replace the large "institutional, task-centered facility" approach with a "people-centered" facility featuring small, ten-twelve person "homes", where each resident has their own private bedroom and their own private bathroom, and each "home" has their own food preparation and dining facility, and their own caregivers. For more information and to locate a Green House facility in your area:
http://thegreenhouseproject.org/

Chapter 11: Advance Directives

What Are Advance Directives?

Advance Directives are a set of legal documents wherein a person spells out their wishes and decisions, regarding end of life treatment, should they become incapacitated and unable to communicate these wishes themselves. Advance Directives are generally comprised of the following documents:

1. Directive to Physicians: Sometimes known as a Living Will, this document allows you to communicate your wishes about Medical Treatment options, should you become unable to make these wishes known because of illness or injury.
2. Declaration for Mental Health Treatment– this document allows you to communicate your wishes about mental health treatment options should you become mentally impaired and unable to communicate these wishes yourself.
3. Medical Power of Attorney – is a document naming some other person to make medical decisions for you, should you become incapacitated and unable to make these decisions for yourself.
4. Out of Hospital Do Not Resuscitate Order – this document contains instructions for Emergency Personnel who might treat you outside of a hospital setting if they arrive and find your heart stopped or if you have stopped breathing.
5. HIPAA Power of Attorney - Naming people who will have access to your medical records and who are authorized to speak with your doctors (in this case, only to obtain and/or share information, not make decisions).
6. Durable Power of Attorney for Finances – is a document naming some other person to make financial decisions for you, should you become incapacitated and unable to make these decisions for yourself.

By making these wishes known in advance, maintaining them in written form, and having them readily accessible, a person is able to remove any uncertainty about their desires; even further, it will avoid any confusion by removing the burden of "decision-making by guess" from family, friends, and/or medical personnel, in the case of serious illness or injury. All of these types of Advance Directives are explained in greater detail below.

Directive to Physicians

The Directive to Physicians is a legal document designed to communicate your wishes about medical treatment that should or should not be administered, if you find yourself in a hospital due to illness or injury, and unable to make your wishes known yourself. Specifically, it allows you to formally declare that:

- You wish to be kept alive, even if in a terminal condition, by any and all available means; **or**
- You want all treatments withheld, other than those needed to keep you comfortable and free of pain, and that you wish to be allowed to die naturally and with dignity.

- Additionally, you also have the option to list any specific treatments that you either do or do not want, such as the administration of antibiotics or intravenous fluids and nutrition.

These are truly life-and-death declarations, based on both your personal life values as well as your spiritual or religious convictions. They are obviously very intimate and personal decisions, and while some people will know their own heart and have very definitive ideas about their end-of-life wishes, others may find these decisions overwhelming and morally challenging, and will need to seek the advice and support from family members, ministers, social workers, and/or psychological counselors.

In order to be valid, the person creating the Directive to Physicians document must be at least 18 years of age, acting of their own free will, and generally must sign the document in the presence of two witnesses. Further, the witnesses generally cannot be:

- Related to the patient by blood or marriage
- Beneficiaries under the *Will* or anyone who would inherit property if the person died without a will
- The attending physician or an employee of the attending physician
- Anyone directly providing patient care
- An officer, director, partner, or business office employee of the health care facility providing treatment, or any employee of the health care parent organization

After completing and signing the document, a copy should be given to your physician with the request that it be made part of your medical records. A copy should also be given to the person who you select to have Medical Power of Attorney for you (see Medical Power of Attorney below).

Please note that this is an extremely important document, containing life and death declarations. Although sample forms are available on the internet, you need to be aware that laws and nuances vary by state. It is highly recommended, therefore, that you seek the advice and guidance of a qualified attorney when creating, and before finalizing this document.

Declaration for Mental Health Treatment

Similar in nature to the Directive to Physicians, the Declaration for Mental Health Treatment allows you to make decisions in advance about mental health treatment, specifically relating to psychoactive medication, convulsive therapy and emergency mental health treatment. As opposed to the Directive to Physicians, however, instructions that you provide in this document will only be followed if a court decides that you are incapacitated and unable to make treatment decisions for yourself; without a decision by a court, you will be considered able to make treatment decisions for yourself.

Like the Directive to Physicians document, the person creating the Declaration for Mental Health Treatment document must be at least 18 years of age, acting of their own free will, and generally must sign the document in the presence of two witnesses. Further, the witnesses generally cannot be:
- Related to the patient by blood or marriage
- Beneficiaries under the *Will* or anyone who would inherit property if the person died without a will
- The attending physician or an employee of the attending physician
- Anyone directly providing patient care
- An officer, director, partner, or business office employee of the health care facility providing treatment, or any employee of the health care parent organization

After completing and signing the document, a copy should be given to your physician with the request that it be made part of your medical records. A copy should also be given to the person who you select to have Medical Power of Attorney for you (see Medical Power of Attorney below).

Please note that this is an extremely important document, and although sample forms are available on the internet, you need to be aware that laws and nuances vary by state. It is highly recommended, therefore, that you seek the advice and guidance of a qualified attorney when creating, and before finalizing this document.

Medical Power of Attorney
The Medical Power of Attorney is a legal document wherein you select and name some other person to act as your "agent" for the purpose of making all healthcare decisions for you, should you become incapable of making these decisions due to illness or injury. In this case, healthcare decisions are those that relate specifically to the administration or withholding of medical care, medical treatment, medical procedure, or medication. While the Medical Power of Attorney covers virtually all healthcare decisions, it only lasts as long as the person is incapable of making their own decisions. In other words, a person could be temporarily incapacitated due to an accident, but after regaining the power to speak for themselves, they regain their right to make their own healthcare related decisions.

It is extremely important to understand that without stating any specific limitations, the Medical Power of Attorney gives an "agent" very wide latitude when consenting to treatment or withholding of treatment on your behalf. The person granting the Power of Attorney, however, has the right and authority to limit their "agent's" decision-making power by specifically spelling out any specific restrictions to that authority.

It is generally not a good idea to name more than one person, or co-agents, as this could lead to confusion or even conflict at a time when immediate, time-critical decisions need to be made; it is a good idea, on the other hand, to nominate at least one alternate "agent", in case your first choice is unavailable or no longer willing to serve as your "agent". In this case, any alternate agent will have the same authority granted to your original agent, but once again, will have no power to act unless the original agent is unable, unwilling, or otherwise unavailable.

You may revoke or amend a Medical Power of Attorney at any time. To revoke a Power of Attorney, you merely need to communicate your intent to your healthcare provider; the communication can be given orally, but a written document, signed and dated will generally avoid any question or confusion.

Similar to the other documents listed above, the person creating the Medical Power of Attorney must be at least 18 years of age, acting of their own free will, and generally must sign the document in the presence of two witnesses. Further, the witnesses generally cannot be:

- The person you have designated as your "agent"
- Related to the patient by blood or marriage
- Beneficiaries under the *Will* or anyone who would inherit property if the person died without a will
- The attending physician or an employee of the attending physician
- Anyone directly providing patient care
- An officer, director, partner, or business office employee of the health care facility providing treatment, or any employee of the health care parent organization

Be aware that laws and nuances vary by state; it is highly recommended that you seek the advice and guidance of a qualified attorney regarding questions and issues relating to this document.

Choosing Your Healthcare "Agent"
Most people will name their spouse, partner, a relative, or a close friend as their healthcare "agent". It is critical, however, that you have absolute faith and trust in the person that you select to be your "agent", that you have discussed your wishes with them, and have their agreement that they will act in strict accordance with your desires. Your "agent" may not agree with all of your wishes, but must completely respect your right to make your own health care choices according to your own personal values and spiritual beliefs.

It is also important to note that unless you state otherwise, your appointment of a spouse to be your health care "agent" will generally dissolve on divorce. Once again, however, laws and nuances vary by state; it is highly recommended that you seek the advice and guidance of a qualified attorney regarding questions and issues relating to this document.

If You Do Not Name a Health Care Agent
If you do not know anyone or have anyone that you would trust to oversee your healthcare, it is not absolutely necessary to name an agent. In fact, it may be better

not to name anyone than to name someone who is not comfortable with the directions you leave or is not likely to vigorously ensure that your wishes are respected.

In this case, then, having your wishes documented in the Directive to Physicians and made part of your medical records will generally ensure that your medical providers will follow your written wishes. Yet to be doubly sure, it is important that you discuss your wishes for medical care with a doctor or a hospital representative who is likely to be involved in providing that care, and be sure that they see and have access to your Directive to Physicians document.

One Final Note

One final note, and this almost goes without saying: it is extremely important that you discuss your wishes that are documented in your Medical Power of Attorney not only with your "agent", but also with all alternate "agents" as well as any other family and friends that may become involved. Having the discussion, and/or making a copy of your Directive to Physicians available to all interested parties is simply the best way to ensure that everyone is aware of both your wishes and who the decision maker will be, in case you become incapacitated and unable to speak for yourself.

Out of Hospital Do Not Resuscitate

An Out of Hospital Do Not Resuscitate (DNR) order contains instructions to Emergency Personnel who might treat you outside of a hospital setting, if you stop breathing or if your heart stops. This order specifically instructs them NOT to use cardiopulmonary resuscitation (CPR), artificial breathing tubes, electric heart shocks, or any other invasive emergency techniques on you. On the other hand, this Out of Hospital DNR order will not have any effect on the treatment of a person who is still breathing and/or whose heart is still beating.

You need also to be aware, however, that first responders, who arrive to help someone in an emergency situation, or Emergency Room staff attending an arriving patient, will typically not know anything about your preferences for treatment. For anyone prone to cardiac or respiratory arrest, then, many states have authorized the use of an Id Bracelet or Necklace, which, when prominently displayed, will be honored by Emergency first responders and Emergency Room staff. A formal, written DNR form, signed by a qualified physician, is generally required in order to obtain one of these Id Bracelets or Necklaces.

In Hospital Do Not Resuscitate

If you are admitted to a hospital, there is another Do Not Resuscitate order that you can complete and sign, and have it included in your medical records. You can generally obtain this form by requesting it from your Physician, a nurse or other health care provider, or hospital social worker.

HIPAA

HIPAA stands for Health Insurance Portability and Accountability Act, a federal law enacted to protect the privacy of personal medical information. It strictly limits the disclosure of your personal medical information to those directly providing care and any others specifically authorized by the individual, such as a spouse, family, and caregivers. It applies to all medical information collected in a hospital, a doctor's office, or any other place that provides healthcare, and additionally applies to insurance companies and any businesses that store and maintain healthcare information for providers.

HIPAA is based on two important principles of patient care: Privacy and Confidentiality. Privacy refers to a person's right to limit who knows what about one's medical condition. It also refers to the right to have conversations about medical care in places where it cannot be overheard by others. Confidentiality, on the other hand, refers to a health care professional's obligation to keep information from being disclosed without the patient's consent, unless required by law or considered necessary for clinical reasons.

Who Is Allowed to See a Patient's Medical Information?

As a general rule, Physicians and other health care professionals can share medical information with family members, caregivers or others directly involved with a patient's care, without a formal HIPAA Power of Attorney, under the following conditions:

- The patient is conscious
- The patient is mentally coherent
- The patient has the opportunity to object or to otherwise limit who can have access to the medical information

If, however, the patient is not conscious, or is otherwise unable to speak for themselves, a decision to share information could become complicated, and in this case, the Physician is required to use good judgment about what is shared and with whom. For this reason, as part of the Advance Directives package, a HIPAA Power of Attorney, completed beforehand and made part of a person's medical record, can save time and avoid confusion.

Why Do Family Caregivers Need Medical Information?

In general, family and caregivers need medical information so they can better manage and care for the patient. For example, a family member or caregiver will probably need to know the names of the medicines the doctor orders, why the doctor thinks the patient needs them, and what side effects to look out for. Additionally, family members or caregivers who fix meals or help with grocery shopping would need to know about the person's dietary restrictions and any other food issues.

Family members and caregivers may need to be involved in conversations about what kind of care the person will need at home. Many patients, no matter how independent, benefit from having family members and caregivers involved in these discussions and decisions, since they are getting medical care because they are sick or injured, and may not be in a stable frame of mind to make clear and effective decisions.

HIPAA Waiver

To avoid any risk that your physician will be unwilling to provide your "agent" with information regarding your health care and medical condition due to federal HIPAA law, you should ensure that there is language in your Medical Power of Attorney that expressly waives the protection offered by HIPAA. This generally takes the form of a waiver of the right to confidentiality, and should also specify that you authorize your doctor to discuss your medical condition with your "agent" or "agents". (Note, however, that the language of HIPAA refers to a "personal representative" rather than to an "agent", so it would be best to ensure that is the language used in your waiver.)

Mental Health Information

HIPAA applies to all information, including mental health information, with the exception of psychotherapy notes, which receive special protections because of the very sensitive nature of the content.

Summary

In summary, then, the following are generally allowed to see and have access to a patient's medical information:

- Doctors can share medical information with nurses, therapists, and other health care professionals on the patient's medical team. This is obviously important for good care and is not affected by HIPAA.
- An individual who has been granted a Healthcare Power of Attorney generally has the right to see and have access to the patient's medical records and other related medical information
- If the patient is not present (such as receiving surgery), is unconscious, delirious, or has dementia, and in the absence of a HIPAA Power of Attorney, then Healthcare providers are required by HIPAA to use good, professional judgment about which family members and/or caregivers should be told what information and involved in which decisions.
- The patient's information may be shared with health insurance, managed Long Term Care plans, and state and federal agencies. This is required for both claims payment and care coordination.

> **Additional Information**
> Some additional information on HIPAA and family caregivers can be found at the following websites:
>
> **Next Step in Care:**
> www.nextstepincare.org/uploads/File/Guides/HIPAA/HIPAA.pdf
> www.nextstepincare.org/uploads/File/consumer_HIPAA.pdf
>
> **US Department of Health and Human Services: Patient's Guide to the HIPAA Privacy Rules:**
> www.hhs.gov/ocr/privacy

Durable Power of Attorney for Finances

As above, if you were to become incapacitated from an illness or an accident, whether for a brief period or even permanently, someone would need to handle your financial affairs for you. Typically, this would include paying your bills, monitoring and making investment decisions, and generally dealing with all other financial matters for you. Obviously, these matters are best handled by someone that you know and choose rather than leaving the decisions up to a court of law.

The Durable Power of Attorney for Finances, then, is the legal document wherein a person can select and name some other person to act as their "agent" for the purpose of making all financial decisions for them, and for handling all financial matters for them, during the period that they are incapable of making their own decisions.

Once again, the person that you name is usually called your "agent". This person does not have to be an attorney or even financial expert, but someone that you trust completely; someone that you can rely on to make the kinds of decisions that you direct; someone who will be responsible for keeping up with all tasks; and someone with a good deal of common sense. As opposed to the Medical Power of Attorney, where authority is limited to medical decisions, the authority granted under the Durable Power of Attorney for Finances strictly pertains to financial matters, and does not authorize this person to make any medical decisions for you.

Your Agent's Responsibilities

It is extremely important that you understand that, similar to the Medical Power of Attorney, and without stating any specific limitations, the Durable Power of Attorney for Finances gives your "agent" extremely wide latitude in dealing with your finances. Having access to all of your financial assets and accounts, your "agent" would be authorized to perform virtually any act with regard to your property and your financial assets. Typical responsibilities of an "agent" would include:

- Having access to your bank account to pay your bills and the ongoing expenses of your family
- Managing and making decisions regarding your investment and retirement accounts
- Filing and paying your taxes
- Hiring Attorneys, CPAs, and other advisors
- Applying for Social Security, Veteran's, and/or other benefits to which you may be entitled

Choose Your Agent Wisely

The person that you select to be your "agent" must fully understand that they are legally required to act in your best interests, to maintain accurate records, to keep your property separate from their own, and to avoid any conflicts of interest. The "agent" is legally bound to act according to all of the terms, conditions and limitations that you spell out in the Durable Power of Attorney for Finances document, yet if you are not able to monitor their activities, there is always the opportunity for misuse of funds or error.

Additionally, your "agent" can legally be paid for their time and expenses out of your assets, if so stipulated in the Durable Power of Attorney for Finances document, but once again without supervision, there is always both an opportunity and potential for abuse.

Asset Protection and Gifting

Certain provisions are generally added to your Durable Power of Attorney for Finances concerning gifting. This could be important for the following reasons:

1. You may decide ahead of time to begin making gifts of your assets to certain people. While this would typically be a function of your Will to be dealt with after your death, you always have the option to begin giving some or all of your assets away while still living, by directing your "agent" to do the gifting.

2. If you need to enter a nursing home and did not take steps to either shelter or give away your financial assets, then all of your assets could be used to pay for nursing home care. As the law currently stands, up to one half of all of your assets can be transferred or gifted, and thus sheltered, if one has a properly drawn Durable Power of Attorney for Finances that permits gifting.

How Many "Agents"

Like the Medical Power of Attorney above, it is generally preferred to name a single person as your "agent" in your Durable Power of Attorney for Finances. Naming multiple people as "co-agents" could cause delays if your agents are not in agreement and could ultimately end up in Court to resolve their conflict.

Also, like the Medical Power of Attorney above, it is highly recommended that you name at least one alternate "agent" in case your primary "agent" becomes unable or unwilling to carry out the duties under your Durable Power of Attorney for

Finances.

When a Financial Power of Attorney Ends
Generally, a Durable Power of Attorney for Finances will end when you die, which means that your "agent's" authority to continue handling any financial affairs also ends. All expenses or any financial decisions that come due after your death, including making funeral or burial arrangements, paying your on-going bills, or making any other financial decisions, will need to be assumed and handled by your Personal Representative*, the person legally appointed to handle your affairs after your death.

A Durable Power of Attorney for Finances will also end if:
- You revoke it or change "agents": so long as you are mentally competent, you can amend or revoke a Durable Power of Attorney for Finances, or replace your "agent" with another person at any time.
- You get a divorce. In some states, if your spouse is your "agent" and you get a divorce, your ex-spouse's authority is automatically terminated. Once again, this is a complex legal issue, and as always, it is highly recommended that you seek the advice and guidance of a qualified attorney regarding all questions and concerns regarding your Durable Power of Attorney for Finances.
- Your "agent" is unable or unwilling to continue. As sometimes happens, an "agent" becomes incapacitated, dies, or moves away and would therefore be unable to continue as your "agent". For this reason, as mentioned above, you should consider naming one or more alternate "agents" to immediately step in, in the absence of your primary "agent".

*Please see the Chapter entitled Wills & Estates for further information on the handling of your financial affairs after your death.

Especially For Caregivers: Having the Discussion
Caregivers often find themselves in the position of having to introduce uncomfortable topics for discussion with an aging or ailing family member. This is especially true, and can be especially difficult, when discussions related to End of Life decisions need to be initiated. Emotions, life values, religious beliefs, and denial – especially denial - all come into play, and make initiating and having these discussions awkward, uncomfortable, and at times, less than fruitful. Yet rather than take the easy way out and ignore the obvious, assistance by someone outside of the family should be considered.

Assistance by Someone Outside of the Family
Sometimes the issues are so emotionally charged for a family, or relationships are so strained, that people are tempted to take the easy way out and ignore the obvious. Yet knowing that sooner or later decisions will need to be made, and knowing that planning facilitates decisions based on forethought and discussion, an alternative to consider is to seek the assistance of someone outside the family:

- Is there a relative or friend of the family who is not immersed in the daily issues who could be called upon to initiate or moderate the dialogue?
- Is there a minister or someone else from your faith community who has the background and training to assist with this process?
- If hospitalized or in hospice, there are usually professionals available to help initiate and direct these discussions.
- Finally, there are trained Social Workers who are available for a fee to initiate, moderate, and assist with this process.

> **Having the Discussion**
>
> Having advance-care and death planning conversations can be extremely difficult, but the consequences of not having these discussions could be even more difficult and burdensome. To assist in this matter, the internet is full of material and self-help tools that seek to guide individuals and their families in talks about the end-of-life process. One such resource is published by the state of Oregon entitled "How to Communicate Caregiving Issues":
>
> **www.oregon.gov/DHS/spwpd/Pages/caregiving/comm.aspx**
>
> Additionally, two other organizations, "Let's Have Dinner and Talk About Death" and "The Conversation Project" have teamed up to challenge Americans to fill their table with comfort food, family, and friends; to break bread and taboos; and to take part in a nation-wide series of interactive dinners with the intent of "transforming the seemingly difficult conversation about death into an intimate shared experience." To find out more about this project visit :
>
> **http://deathoverdinner.org/**

Other Documents to Consider

Two additional documents that may need to be considered (depending on individual circumstances) are:

- Declaration of Guardian Before Need Arises
- Appointment for Disposition of Remains

Each of these documents is further explained below.

Declaration of Guardian Before Need Arises

Adult Guardianship essentially is a court ordered caretaker relationship whereby an cognitively incapacitated adult has some or all of his or her legal rights removed and given to a guardian who has the legal duty to exercise those rights for the best interest and welfare of the individual. In this case, the court effectively transfers the responsibility for managing finances, living arrangements and medical decisions to the guardian. As you can see, a guardianship is a very serious matter in that it strips an individual of some very fundamental rights and privileges.

It is also important to realize that a spouse or child of an incapacitated adult does not automatically become the guardian upon incapacity; it is generally up to the court to decide unless the individual has stipulated their desires in advance. This is generally done through a simple form called the Declaration of Guardian Before Need Arises, and spells out two very important things:

- Who they desire to be named as their Guardian (primary and successors); and, maybe equally as important:
- Who they specifically <u>do not</u> want to be their Guardian

Note: If someone is appointed as a Guardian, and the incapacitated person already has agents named under a Durable Power of Attorney and/or a Health Care Advance Directive, the court will generally have to determine whether the agent's authority will continue or be replaced by the Guardian.

As you can see, this situation can get to be very complicated, and it is best to seek experienced legal advice prior to any need for a Guardianship.
Source: David R. Brewer, Houston, Texas: www.brewer-law.com

Appointment for Disposition of Remains
The issue of who has the authority to decide whether a person will be cremated or buried becomes especially important when there is a chance that the decedent's family has very set ideas on how their loved one should be honored and remembered, and if those plans run contrary to:

- A long-time or live-in (but unmarried) partner
- A fiancé (or fiancée)
- The decedent's own last wishes

While a *Will* is sometimes an appropriate means for stating these wishes, the *Will* may not be available (or may be contested) at the most critical time when these decisions need to be made. This is where a fully executed and notarized Appointment for Disposition of Remains document will ensure that the decedent's own last wishes will be carried out.

Note that while the basic document specifically appoints an agent to be the authority and make these decisions, the document may also contain a range of written instructions such as burial or cremation, where the remains shall be buried or where the ashes shall be scattered after cremation, budget for a memorial service or funeral, as well as the type of ceremony to be performed (religious, etc.). Once again, this situation can get to be very complicated, and it is best to seek experienced legal advice for completing this and all other related legal documents.

Source: David R. Brewer, Attorney at Law, PLLC, Houston, Texas
www.brewer-law.com

Chapter 12: Wills & Estates

Distribution of Assets after Death

You may be surprised to realize that a *Will* may not be the final decider of how certain assets are distributed after a person's death; depending on the type of asset, the following hierarchy will generally determine how/to whom these assets will typically be distributed:

- Direct Transfer to named Beneficiary or Beneficiaries
- Joint Ownership
- Trust Ownership
- *Will* and/or Probate

What this means, for example, is that should there be a conflict between a person's wishes as spelled out in their *Will* and a Beneficiary named on an account, the named Beneficiary would take precedence and inherit the account. Additionally, some types of ownership will allow assets to be transferred easily and without tax consequences, while other types of ownership may require months, have tax consequences, and require the assistance of an Attorney and/or a Financial Advisor.

This Chapter, while not intended to be a substitute for competent legal or financial advice, will provide an explanation of some key legal and financial concepts that will help you to understand why planning ahead is so critically important and will assist you when working with your legal and financial advisors.

What is an Estate?

An Estate is simply the legal entity created as a result of a person's death. The Estate consists of all the property or assets, whether real or personal, owned by a person at the time of death. As a legal entity, the estate is responsible for paying any debts owed by the decedent and then distributing the balance of the estate's assets to the beneficiaries named in either the *Will* or through the Probate process. This approach applies generally to all assets covered by the *Will* or owned by the Estate, but certain other types of assets can be distributed directly to the beneficiaries, bypassing this process. Assets that bypass the Estate are described in detail in the paragraph below entitled **Direct Transfer Assets**.

Executors, Administrators, and Personal Representatives

A Personal Representative is the general term used to describe the person in charge of handling the affairs of a decedent's estate. Two other terms are important to understand: the first is *Executor*, which refers to the person named in the *Will*, to be in charge of handling the affairs of the decedent's estate; the other is *Administrator*, which refers to the person named by the Probate Court, to be in charge of handling the affairs of the decedent's estate, when a decedent has died without a *Will*. For the sake of brevity, the term Personal Representative will be used inclusively throughout this text, to refer to either an Executor or an Administrator.

What is a Will?
A *Will* is a legal document, created while a person is living, giving instructions for the distribution of that person's assets after death. Typically, it details:
- Who will get what assets
- How they will get them
- When they will get them

It will also name one or more Personal Representatives, who are the people responsible for managing the estate and the distribution of assets. If there is a valid *Will*, the Estate is referred to by the legal term **testate**. Not all people who die, however, have had the opportunity to create a *Will* ahead of time. In this case, you will hear the term **intestate**, which is the legal term that means "dying without a *Will*".

So, what happens if a person dies without a *Will*? In some cases, as in a Community Property state such as Texas, all asset ownership would automatically be transferred to the surviving spouse, if there is one; and if the total value of all of the assets is under the current Federal Estate Tax limits, there may not be a need to go through the Probate process (the legal process further described below), and there may not be any Estate Taxes due. In non-Community Property states, or in Community Property states where there is no surviving spouse, the assets will be distributed by the court according to the legal formula enacted by that particular state.

In any case, the laws are subject to change from year to year, so, whether the person died with or without a *Will*, or whether or not Estate Taxes will be due, are questions best left to your professional tax or legal advisors.

Additional Questions
After reading the above paragraphs, some additional questions may come immediately to mind:
- Do I need a *Will*?
- Do I already have a *Will*, and if I do, is it current?
- Where is the best place to store a *Will*?

The following sections will address these questions in further detail.

Do I Need a Will?
The simplest answer to this question is: "It depends". Are you married or single? Do you have children? Do you have children from a prior marriage? Do you live in a Community Property state? How large is your estate? Are there any special people in your life that you will want to leave certain gifts to or maybe a charitable organization that you will want to remember with a financial gift?

As you can see, each situation is highly personal and so the best and most practical answer is to seek guidance and counsel from a qualified attorney who specializes in Estates, Wills, and Probate matters. Generally, an initial consultation will be complimentary.

If I Have a *Will*

If you already have a *Will*, chances are it is not current. With the passage of time, everyone's situation will change, and can result in outdated and inaccurate information that could potentially cause unneeded complications should you die prior to having the *Will* updated. Some of the most common problems with outdated *Wills* are:

- Marital Status change
- Child is born or adopted
- Children are older and no longer need a Guardian
- Newer, intended recipients never recorded
- *Will* location is forgotten

Where to Store a *Will*

Not being able to locate a *Will* after a death can be the source of great anxiety and frustration to your loved ones, and can also create potential legal problems should there be a dispute over inherited assets. There are several theories on the best place to store a *Will*; these are described below, however each could have a critical disadvantage as described in the following paragraph:

- In Safety Deposit Box at a bank
- In an attorney's office
- In a fireproof safe in your home
- In the possession of your Personal Representative
- In digital form in one of the many online services (ie: on the server of an online service provider, where it can be encrypted, stored, and backed up by the service, away from the hard drive of your personal computer.

In most cases, a surviving spouse or one of the heirs will have knowledge of where your *Will* is stored and have access to it. However, please be aware that none of the above approaches, in and of themselves, are perfect and could cause unneeded complications to a grieving family after a death:

- If a *Will* is stored in a Safety Deposit Box, registered in the name of a decedent alone, additional complications can occur, since only the registered owner will be given access to the box by the bank. In this case, an heir or beneficiary named in the *Will* would not have immediate access to the box, and would generally need a Court order for the bank to open and search the box.
- With the passage of time, attorneys could retire, join other firms, leave the area, or otherwise become difficult to locate; and further, with the passage of time, you could lose contact with or even forget the attorney's name or firm.
- A lost key or combination to a fireproof safe would require the services of a locksmith and is another unneeded complication and expense, at a very inconvenient time.
- Your Personal Representative could become incapacitated or even die without leaving instructions with someone else as to where your documents are stored.

- Documents stored online will need a password to allow access, and without the password, accessing the documents will be difficult or even impossible.

Obviously, this is not a perfect world, so it may be appropriate to consider redundant storage and/or redundant knowledge of the whereabouts of the document: having copies of the document stored in multiple places, with two or more trusted people having knowledge of, and access to the storage locations of your document.

Who to Choose as Executor

As mentioned above, an *Executor*, or Personal Representative, is the person named in the *Will* who will be in charge of handling the affairs of a decedent's estate. Before addressing the question of "who to select", however, it might be helpful to review some of their major duties and responsibilities:

- Selecting an attorney (if an attorney has not been pre-selected), and overseeing the probate process (further defined in the section below).
- Locating and making a complete inventory of all assets in the estate.
- Gaining access to the funds of the estate to pay bills, including funeral expenses.
- Preparing and Filing the final income tax returns.
- Distributing or overseeing the distribution of all assets to the beneficiaries named in the *Will*.

While most people think first of naming a spouse, family member, or close friend, it is important to realize that, given all the responsibility, the ideal candidate should be someone who is well-organized, dependable, honest, good with paperwork and vigilant about meeting deadlines.

In the event that you do not have a relative or friend that you feel comfortable with, you can make an arrangement with a bank or a professional in your area that has experience in dealing with Wills and estates.

For specific assistance in locating a professional in your area:
- National Association of Estate Planners and Councils:
    www.naepc.org
- National Academy of Elder Law Attorneys:
    www.naela.org

The above organizations merely provide directories on their websites to help you find a professional in your area; they do not make recommendations. For more information on finding and hiring a professional, please refer to a later Chapter entitled "Hiring Professional Advisors".

Executor Fees
Most family members and close friends (especially if they are a beneficiary) will perform the duties of Executor or Personal Representative for free, but if the estate is large and complicated, or you elect to use a third party, be aware that it will cost the estate. Professional fees are generally set by each state and are typically in the 1% to 5% range of the total value of the estate. If you have any questions regarding Executor fees or any other aspect of *Wills* and Estates, you will need to seek legal advice and counsel from a qualified attorney who specializes in Wills, Trusts, Estates, and/or Elder law.

What is Probate?
Probate is the legal process pertaining to the administration of an Estate after a death, since the assets in the estate must be disbursed in a certain manner: ie: all debts and taxes must be paid first, prior to distributing the remainder to the heirs.

Note: the term **Heir** specifically refers to a decedent's blood relatives such as children, siblings, and parents, as well as the decedent's spouse. There are other legal terms for individuals who are not directly related to the decedent, but for the purpose of this book, the term H*eir* will be used to refer to anyone named to inherit in a *Will*.

In a Community Property state, such as Texas, the law recognizes a married couple's property as jointly owned; if a person dies *intestate*, the portion of the estate jointly owned will generally pass to a surviving spouse without the requirement for probate, unless the decedent had children from a prior marriage. Once again, it is important to seek legal advice and counsel from an attorney who specializes in *Wills*, Trusts, and Estate law to understand all of your legal rights and responsibilities.

Direct Transfer Assets
Certain types of assets allow the direct transfer to a new owner when the current owner dies, if the asset has a named beneficiary, a *Payable-On-Death*, or *Transfer-On-Death* provision. Life Insurance policies are a primary example of a Direct Transfer asset, as are some bank deposit and CD accounts and certain Brokerage, Investment, and Retirement accounts, with *Payable-On-Death* or *Transfer-on-Death* provisions. Certain assets owned jointly also fall under this category. Direct Transfer assets generally pass tax-free to the beneficiary, although taxes may be required on any interest or income earned after the decedent's date of death.

As in all cases, it is important to seek the guidance of a qualified professional to ensure that all beneficiaries are current and properly documented for all assets eligible for Direct Transfer after a death, to avoid any problems in assuming ownership or taking any distributions from any inherited accounts.

What is a Trust?
A Trust is a legal means for controlling the management of certain property and assets while a person is alive, and for directing and controlling the distribution of certain assets after a death. In other words, they are set up for the management of

certain assets upon incapacity of the owner, or to minimize Estate Taxes and pass ownership upon death without the need for Probate. This type of trust is known as a *Living Trust*. Another form of Trust is a *Testamentary Trust*, created through the *Will* of a deceased person, and is generally used to protect and distribute assets to heirs who may not be able or are not quite ready to handle large sums of money on their own.

As part of the Trust process, a Trustee is named (an individual or an institution) that will be responsible for overseeing the management of all the assets owned by the Trust.

A couple of examples may be useful in illustrating the use of a *Trust*. In the case of a *Living Trust*, aging parents may set up this type of trust and transfer ownership of their home and other assets into the trust. Should they become incapacitated, the Trust can protect their assets from creditors and the Trustee can continue to manage the property and continue managing and paying the bills. In the case of a *Testamentary Trust*, parents may not want minor children inheriting large sums of money, so this type of Trust is set up that will allow a Trustee to manage the inheritance until the minor children reach a certain age.

In any case, Estates involving a Trust can be simple or complex, but it is always advisable to seek the guidance and counsel of a qualified Attorney to ensure that you understand all of your duties, rights and responsibilities, whenever a Trust is involved.

When is Trust Better than *Will*

1. A Trust can be used to avoid Probate;
2. A Trust can provide Creditor Protection for the heirs' inheritance against claims against the heirs;
3. A Trust can protect Government Benefits for a person with Disabilities;
4. A Trust can reduce Estate Taxes;
5. A Trust can administer benefits to minor beneficiaries without court intervention

As noted above, it is always advisable to seek the guidance and counsel of a qualified Attorney to ensure that you understand which option is best for you and your heirs

Community Property
For those with a traditional marriage, dying without a *Will* in a Community Property state such as Texas might not be as serious a problem as one might imagine. For the traditional marriage, one with a surviving spouse and no children from a previous marriage, ownership of all assets will generally pass to the surviving spouse; and when the surviving spouse passes away, all of the assets are divided equally among the surviving children. For most people, this is exactly the plan that they already had in mind.

Issues arise, however, for families with children from previous marriages. The state will typically be concerned about the welfare of the decedent's children if all of the assets should go to the surviving spouse. Thus, it is typical for the state to award half of the assets to any surviving children, even if the children are being cared for by the surviving spouse. Think about this: half of the assets would mean half of the house, half of all the money in the bank accounts, and half of the decedent's Pension and Retirement accounts. This is an instance where matters could get complicated very quickly, and would need to be one of the first questions that you should discuss with a qualified attorney.

Keeping Your *Will* Current
At this point it should be obvious that planning ahead is always preferable to dealing with a problem after the fact. If you do not have a *Will*, or if your *Will* is out of date, now would be the time to consider having a new *Will* created or an out-of-date *Will* updated, while the topic is still fresh in your mind. Don't leave the task of second-guessing your wishes, or conflict resolution, to grieving loved ones after your death.

One final note about keeping your *Will* current: some *Wills* contain general language in the body of the document, and further contain appendices naming both specific assets and the person to whom they will go. As time passes, the *Will*-owner could make changes to the appendices, and confusion after a death could occur if appendices are not properly dated and signed. The point is that any changes to the appendices should be properly dated and initialed or signed, and the earlier, out of date appendices should be re-called and destroyed.

Professional Assistance
As will be repeated over and over again in this text, it is highly recommended that you seek the advice of a qualified Financial Advisor, Attorney, and/or a CPA to ensure that:
- All documents are properly drawn;
- All legal, tax, and financial consequences are fully understood; and
- All documents are in compliance with the laws of your state.

If you do not have an Attorney, CPA, or Financial Advisor, please refer to the Chapter on Hiring Professional Advisors later in this text.

Watch those Beneficiary Designations

For estates with multiple heirs/beneficiaries, it is extremely important for everyone to understand that there are two ways that property can be distributed after a death: **Pro Rata** and **Per Stirpes**. Which designation used is not particularly important if all beneficiaries are alive at the testator's (person making the *Will*) death, but problems could arise if one of the beneficiaries predeceases the testator. The following example will highlight the differences:

For this example, let's assume a family consisting of a single parent and three adult children. The intent is for all three adult children to share equally the proceeds of the estate at the death of the parent. If the parent dies first, all three adult children will be entitled to one-third of the proceeds. If one of the children predeceases the parent, then the following rules would generally apply:

- If the beneficiary designation is Pro Rata: the remaining two adult children would each be entitled to **one-half** of the proceeds at the parent's death. This could be a problem if the deceased child had a family: the family would in effect be disinherited and not be entitled to receive any of the proceeds from the estate.
- If the beneficiary designation is Per Stirpes: the estate would continue to be split in thirds: the remaining two adult children would each be entitled to one-third of the proceeds, and the family of the deceased adult child would likewise be entitled to one-third of the proceeds.

To further complicate matters under a Per Stirpes designation, children from prior marriages could also be entitled to share in the proceeds. It is, as always, highly recommended that you seek the advice of a qualified Financial Advisor, Attorney, and/or CPA to ensure that your wishes for distributing your assets are clearly spelled out.

Chapter 13: Hiring Professional Advisors

Hiring Professional Advisors

Most people do not have a team of Legal, Tax, Healthcare, and Financial Advisors in place, standing by to help and assist in dealing with each of the various aspects of Eldercare, End-of-Life, and After-Death affairs. If you are like most of us, and do not have this team already in place, this chapter will help you understand the role that each of these professionals will play, why you will need them, how they may be able to assist you, and finally, a list of questions to ask each of them before you make your hiring decision.

Financial Advisor

In general, the term Financial Advisor can refer to a variety of professionals from Stock Brokers, to Insurance Agents, to Financial Advisors and Financial Planners. For the purpose of this text, however, the term Financial Advisor will be used to refer only to those professionals with more than a single focus, ie: more than just the selling of insurance or the selling of investments. In other words, the ideal Financial Advisor would be an independent advisor who will have access to virtually all investment and all insurance products from all of the best companies on the market today.

Why Do You Need a Financial Advisor?

It is generally obvious why you might need an Attorney or a CPA, but the reasons may not be so obvious when it comes to a Financial Advisor. So, why would you need one?

While an attorney is obviously the best qualified person to assist you in dealing with legal aspects, and a CPA is the best qualified to assist you in dealing with tax aspects, an experienced and qualified Financial Advisor (as defined above) will:

- Have both a broad as well as an in-depth knowledge of all types of Investment Products
- Be able to offer advice on alternative types of investments tailored to fit your specific needs and circumstances
- Be able to offer advice on the appropriate strategies for structuring the ownership and beneficiary arrangements for your accounts
- Be able to offer advice on the suitable strategies for structuring withdrawals when the time comes

In short, a qualified and experienced Financial Advisor is in the best position to offer direction and advice on limiting tax consequences and maximizing benefits from virtually all investment and insurance products, and further, a qualified and experienced Financial Advisor can be a great quarterback for your entire team of advisors, as there is likely to be both legal and tax implications throughout the life cycle of most investment products, and perhaps even more so after a death.

Financial Advisor Compensation
Before you select a Financial Advisor, it is critical that you understand how the Financial Advisor expects to be paid. Unlike Attorneys and CPAs, however, Financial Advisors can be compensated in a variety of ways:

- **Hourly Rate**: As the title implies, the Financial Advisor will charge you a set hourly rate for all the time that is spent on your work. There are generally no other filing fees or administrative expenses associated with the advisory portion of this work, however, there may be commissions to be paid if the work involves the purchase or sale of stock or other investment products. As always, it is a good practice to ask for an overall or most conservative estimate of the total costs that you can expect to pay to avoid any unpleasant surprises when the bills arrive.
- **Commissions** for buying and selling individual stocks and bonds: if either a purchase or sale of individual stocks or bonds is involved, you will be responsible for a commission on each transaction. Typically, commissions will be deducted from the proceeds of the transaction. Commission schedules can vary between Advisors, so as a reminder, it is always a good practice to understand any proposed commission structure prior to the execution of any financial transactions.
- **Commissions** for the purchase of Insurance products, and various other Investment products, are typically paid by the companies that market the products; while you will not be paying these commissions out of your pocket, the companies will be charging fees that will be deducted in one form or another from your portfolio.
- Some Financial Advisors charge an **Annual Percentage** of the total portfolio, for the management of the portfolio. Once again, it is a good practice to understand any proposed fee structure prior to making any final commitments.
- Many Financial Planners will want to create a complete Financial Plan for you prior to taking you on as a client. While the Financial Plan is a sound approach for documenting where you stand now, financially, and where you want to be, financially, and for use in guiding the selection of various investment vehicles, be aware that the cost can vary from a few hundred dollars to well over a thousand dollars. Once again, ask questions and understand any proposed fee structure prior to making any final commitments.
- Sometimes a Financial Planner may want to charge one fee structure for a certain portion of your portfolio, and another fee structure for the other portion. At the risk of sounding too repetitive, ask questions and understand all proposed fee structures prior to making any final commitments.

Important Questions to Ask

- ✓ What is your particular specialty and how much overall experience do you have?
- ✓ How much experience do you have in dealing with people in my circumstances?
- ✓ Are you limited in the number and types of products that you can offer me and why?
- ✓ Are you properly licensed or registered by both the state and federal authorities?
- ✓ What specific services will you be providing and why will I need them?
- ✓ Do you foresee any problems with this case?
- ✓ Have you had any sanctions or disciplinary measures (or look this up ahead of time yourself)?
- ✓ What is the total cost that I can expect to pay, and how is that broken down?
- ✓ Do I feel comfortable working with this Advisor– is everything explained in terms that I can easily understand and have all of my questions been answered to my satisfaction?

Licensing, Education, Designations, and Experience

First, a word about licenses: it is important to understand that not all financial advisors can represent all types of investments. To be more specific: a Series 6 registration, for example, is known as a limited investment securities registration, and restricts the holder to selling limited types of investments such as mutual funds. A Series 7 registration, on the other hand, is known as a general securities registration, and allows the holder to sell a broader range of securities, including individual stocks and bonds, as well as mutual fund products. Beyond that, there are various other products, such as variable annuities, which require both a securities registration and an insurance license to market and sell. The overall point here, then, is that not all advisors have invested the time and effort to acquire the knowledge and obtain the registrations and the licenses required to represent the entire range of investment products; and lack of access to all available products could have the potential to seriously impact the advice that will be provided.

A second point to consider in selecting an advisor is formal education. Certain designations, such as BA (Bachelor of Arts; typically a four year college degree), MBA (Master of Business Administration; typically two additional years of college training beyond the original four years), and JD (Juris Doctor; a law degree from an accredited university), for example, will let you know how much formal education a person has obtained. Just as you would expect your dentist to have a college degree and have completed Dental school, so too, should you expect nothing less education-wise when selecting a financial advisor with whom you will be entrusting your life savings.

And last, but certainly not least, would be industry experience. Even with all of the registrations, with an advanced degree, and with multiple industry designations, the advisor you should consider choosing is probably the one with a combination of education, credentials, and number of years of actual experience in the practice of the profession, along with a personal comfort level with the actual person. It's your life savings we are talking about; would you really be willing to be a financial guinea pig?

How to Find a Qualified Financial Advisor

There are numerous ways to find a Financial Advisor who has experience in the area of either retired and/or deceased persons. Among the best ways are:

- Get a referral from one of your other trusted advisors such as your attorney, CPA, or banker; typically these advisors work with one or more Financial Advisors and are in a good position to make a recommendation with confidence.
- Get a referral from family or friends; ask around; having someone you know and trust, who has used a Financial Advisor with this type of experience and were happy with the services, is also a very good option.
- The State or Local Certified Financial Planning Associations will provide a list of Financial Planners in your area, but will not be able to make a recommendation.
- The Internet is maybe the last place to look, but Financial Planners who have a presence on the internet will typically post enough information about their services to allow you to make some initial selections.

Note: there are numerous designations and certifications that a Financial Advisor might attain, but the most important thing to look for generally turns out to be years of successful experience and expertise, as education designations and certifications alone are never guarantees of competency.

Questions about an Advisor or Firm?

FINRA, the Financial Industry Regulatory Authority has an online data base available to the public, called Broker/Check.

For individual brokers, Broker/Check will tell you:
- Where the broker works currently
- The broker's employment history for the past 10 years, in and outside the brokerage industry
- What licenses the broker holds and where the broker is registered
- The qualification exams the broker has passed

Broker/Check also will tell you whether the broker has been:
- Charged or convicted of any criminal felonies
- Charged or convicted of any investment-related misdemeanors
- Subject to any industry disciplinary actions or investigations by regulators
- Involved in any investment-related civil actions or proceedings
- Named in any consumer-initiated complaints, arbitration proceedings, or civil law suits
- Cited for failing to pay judgments or liens
- In bankruptcy proceedings
- Terminated by an employer following allegations of misconduct or failing to supervise subordinates

FINRA Disciplinary Actions Online
In addition to Broker/Check, FINRA has a separate database for viewing FINRA's disciplinary actions against brokers. You can search for cases and actions back to 2006 that are eligible for publication pursuant to FINRA Rule 8313 (Release of Disciplinary Complaints, Decisions and Other Information). You can search the FINRA Disciplinary Actions Online by individual name, firm name, case number, date range, document type, document text, or CRD number. Results will include opinions issued by the SEC and federal appellate courts that relate to FINRA disciplinary actions that have been appealed.

Source for the above, and to access Broker/Check:
https://brokercheck.finra.org/
(As of 4-11-2018)

Finding the Right Attorney

Two types of attorney specializations are perhaps the most relevant to this section: Estate Planning attorneys and Elder Care attorneys. On the surface, it might seem that there is little or no distinction between these two types of attorneys, yet in reality:

- An Estate Planning attorney generally focuses on how to protect and distribute your assets after your death
- An Elder Care attorney generally focuses on how to protect your assets while you are still living

To be more specific, an Estate Planning attorney generally deals with the creation of legal documents and vehicles, such as *Wills* and Trusts, to help minimize taxes and expenses while ensuring that your assets are distributed according to your wishes after your death. Elder Care attorneys, on the other hand, typically concentrate on a broader range of legal issues confronting seniors, including planning for aging, illness, and incapacity, along with the complexities involved in qualifying for Medicaid and Veterans coverage for Long Term Care.

Attorney Compensation

Before you select an attorney, you should understand how the attorney expects to be paid. Typically, there are three approaches (note that this is a general overview; some states actually limit the way an attorney can be compensated due to ethical issues associated with the different methods of payment):

- **Flat Fee**: A flat fee is basically a fixed price for doing the work, but generally covers only the attorney's time. In addition to the attorney's time, you can expect to pay any fees involved in court filings, recording costs, and various other out of pocket costs such as appraisals, postage, and etc. It is always a good practice to ask for an overall or most conservative estimate of the total costs that you can expect to pay to avoid any unpleasant surprises when the bills arrive.
- **Hourly Rate**: As the title implies, the attorney will charge you a set hourly rate for all the time that is spent on your work. Additionally, you can expect to pay all additional fees involved in court filings, recording costs, and various other out of pocket costs such as appraisals, postage, and etc. Hourly rates vary greatly from attorney to attorney, and it is always a good practice to ask for an overall or most conservative estimate of the total costs that you can expect to pay to avoid any unpleasant surprises when the bills arrive.
- **Percentage of Estate Value**: specifically related to a Probate matter, some attorneys may charge a percentage of the total value of all of the assets in the estate. This is generally not the most desirable option because it could be the most costly. Once again, it is always a good practice to ask for an overall or most conservative estimate of the total costs that you can expect to pay to avoid any unpleasant surprises when the bills arrive.

Many attorneys will make the time for an initial consultation free of charge. At the initial meeting you will be able to ask some general questions about the attorney's background and experience, and have an opportunity to understand how the attorney charges for this type of work. You may want to interview two or three attorneys to compare background, experience, services to be rendered, and understand the costs you will be paying, prior to making a final decision.

Important Questions to Ask
- ✓ Does your practice focus specifically on Elder Care or Estates, Wills, Trusts, and Probate matters?
- ✓ What specific experience and expertise do you have in regard to our particular matter?
- ✓ Are you certified in the area of expertise we are seeking: Certified Elder Law Attorney, National Academy of Elder Law Attorneys, or Board Certified in Estate Planning?
- ✓ How many years of experience do you have in this specific specialty?
- ✓ Are you properly licensed in this state?
- ✓ What specific services will you be providing and why will I need them?
- ✓ Do you foresee any problems with this case?
- ✓ Have you had any sanctions or disciplinary measures (or look this up online ahead of time yourself)?
- ✓ What is the total cost that I can expect to pay, and how is that broken down?
- ✓ Do I feel comfortable working with this attorney – is everything explained in terms that I can easily understand and have all of my questions been answered to my satisfaction?

How to Find a Qualified Attorney
There are numerous ways to find an attorney who specializes in Wills, Estate, and Probate law. Among the best ways are:
- Get a referral from one of your other trusted advisors such as your CPA, Financial Advisor, or banker; typically these advisors work with one or more attorneys and are in a good position to make a recommendation with confidence.
- Get a referral from family or friends; ask around; having someone you know and trust, who has used this type of attorney and were happy with the services, is also a very good option.
- The State Bar will provide a list of attorneys in your area who specialize in this type of law, but will not be able to make a recommendation.
- The Internet is maybe the last place to look, but attorneys who have a presence on the internet will typically post enough information about their services to allow you to make some initial selections.

Note: finding an attorney through a trusted advisor or someone you know will always give you the most confidence; if you choose to use the State Bar or even the internet, however, you might want to ensure that the attorney whom you select is **Board Certified** in this area of specialty.

> **Legal Issues that Caregivers Face**
>
> All too often the elderly are taken advantage of, and more often than we care to imagine, it is not by a stranger, by a member of their own family. The following are a few of the topic headlines from the Message Board on AgeingCare.com; they make interesting but sobering reading:
> - My brother is stealing money from our elderly mother
> - Mom never changed her Power of Attorney and now she has advanced Alzheimer's
> - My mother turned me and my siblings in for elder abuse
> - My siblings only care about their inheritance, not Mom's well being
> - My elderly mother is being taken advantage of by a younger man
>
> www.agingcare.com/Articles/caregiver-legal-battles-elder-care-issues-139138.htm

Certified Public Accountants (CPA)

Many of us have been preparing our own taxes with the help of popular software programs such as Turbo-Tax, while a number of others might be using the tax preparation services at the local shopping center. While this approach will generally serve you well under normal circumstances, it might be wise for you to seek the assistance of a Certified Public Accountant (CPA) when dealing with the situation of a death. Most state boards of accountancy require a minimum of 150 hours of additional university education, from an accredited institution – which typically equates to a Master's degree – along with a minimum number of college credits in various accounting topics and business law, in order to qualify to sit for the CPA exam. Additionally, each state typically mandates that all CPAs remain current on changes to the tax code laws by taking Continuing Education Courses each and every year. Finally, the tax laws regarding death are subject to change, and it is extremely important that you have the most up-to-date advice when dealing with both estate and inheritance tax situations.

CPA Compensation

Before you select a CPA, it is critical that you understand how the CPA expects to be paid. Typically, there are two approaches:

- **Flat Fee**: A flat fee is basically a fixed price for doing the entire project, or a specified fee for completing each tax return. Unlike the situation with attorneys, there are generally no other filing fees or administrative expenses associated with your tax work. It is always a good practice, however, to ask for an overall or most conservative estimate of the total costs that you can expect to pay to avoid any unpleasant surprises when the bills arrive.

- **Hourly Rate**: As the title implies, the CPA will charge you a set hourly rate for all the time that is spent on your work. Again, as mentioned in the flat fee option, there are generally no other filing fees or administrative expenses associated with your tax work, however, as always, it is a good practice to ask for an overall or most conservative estimate of the total costs that you can expect to pay to avoid any unpleasant surprises when the bills arrive.

Fees and hourly rates vary greatly from CPA to CPA, so you may want to interview two or three to compare background, experience, services to be rendered, and understand the costs you will be paying, prior to making a final decision.

Important Questions to Ask
- ✓ How much experience do you have in the area of Wills, Estates and filings for deceased persons?
- ✓ Are you properly licensed in this state?
- ✓ What specific services will you be providing and why will I need them?
- ✓ Do you foresee any problems with this case?
- ✓ Have you had any sanctions or disciplinary measures (or look this up online ahead of time yourself)?
- ✓ What is the total cost that I can expect to pay, and how is that broken down?
- ✓ Do I feel comfortable working with this CPA – is everything explained in terms that I can easily understand and have all of my questions been answered to my satisfaction?

How to Find a Qualified CPA
There are numerous ways to find a CPA who has experience in the area of Wills, Estates, Eldercare, and filings for deceased persons. Among the best ways are:
- Get a referral from one of your other trusted advisors such as your attorney, Financial Advisor, or banker; typically these advisors work with one or more CPAs and are in a good position to make a recommendation with confidence.
- Get a referral from family or friends; ask around; having someone you know and trust, who has used this type of CPA and were happy with the services, is also a very good option.
- The State or Local CPA Associations will provide a list of CPAs in your area, but will not be able to make a recommendation.
- The Internet is maybe the last place to look, but CPAs who have a presence on the internet will typically post enough information about their services to allow you to make some initial selections.

Smart Retirement

Final Words

As mentioned in the beginning of this text, it was originally written to accompany a live seminar of the same name, although the information is formatted and presented in such a way that it can be read and used as a stand-alone reference manual. In either event, the goal is to both inform and remind – to create a single, comprehensive reference for assisting everyone in creating their own successful retirement.

For information about upcoming seminars, please contact the author at:

Tom Stephens
(713) 416-0157
tom@tsswealth.com

Smart Retirement

Smart Retirement

Appendix Section

---

1. Key Personal Information
2. Emergency Contact Information
3. Legal and Financial Advisors
4. Legal Documents: Checklist & Location
5. Funeral Wishes and Pricing Worksheet
6. Spending Plan Template
7. Texas Advance Directives Forms
8. Starting the End of Life Conversation
9. Life Expectancy Calculators
10. Medicare Summary of Costs
11. Social Security Retirement Age Information
12. Quality of Life Exercises

The Worksheets contained in this Appendix are intended to be used in place: that is, you can fill in the blanks right on the pages of this book and then retain this book along with all other important legal and financial documents (ie: Advance Directives, Will, and etc.). Alternatively, individual pages can be photocopied and then maintained in a separate file, again, stored with all other important legal and financial documents. Please remember that sensitive personal and personally identifying information will be recorded in these worksheets and they need to be safeguarded along with all other legal and financial documents.

Note: The information presented is for general information only, and is not intended to be a substitute for specific, individualized tax, legal, or financial advice. We suggest that you discuss your specific situation with a qualified tax, legal, and/or financial advisor.

Smart Retirement

Smart Retirement

KEY PERSONAL INFORMATION

Name: _____

Date of Birth: _____

Social Security Number: _____

Medicare Insurance Number: _____

Driver License Number: _____

Email Address: _____

Online Accounts

Account	Username	Password
_____	_____	_____
_____	_____	_____
_____	_____	_____
_____	_____	_____
_____	_____	_____
_____	_____	_____
_____	_____	_____
_____	_____	_____
_____	_____	_____
_____	_____	_____

Appendix 1

Smart Retirement

EMERGENCY CONTACT INFORMATION

Family and Friends

Name: _____ Phone: _____

Name: _____ Phone: _____

Name: _____ Phone: _____

Name: _____ Phone: _____

Name: _____ Phone: _____

Name: _____ Phone: _____

Medical and Financial

Medical Power of Attorney

Name: _____ Phone: _____

Financial Power of Attorney

Name: _____ Phone: _____

Employer/Supervisor

Name: _____ Phone: _____

Other Employer Contact

Name: _____ Phone: _____

Clergy

Name: _____ Phone: _____

Smart Retirement

Physicians

Specialty: _____

Name: _____ **Phone:** _____

Specialty: _____

Name: _____ **Phone:** _____

Specialty: _____

Name: _____ **Phone:** _____

Specialty: _____

Name: _____ **Phone:** _____

Specialty: _____

Name: _____ **Phone:** _____

Specialty: _____

Name: _____ **Phone:** _____

Smart Retirement

LEGAL AND FINANCIAL ADVISORS

Attorney

Name: _____   **Phone:** _____

Financial Advisor

Name: _____   **Phone:** _____

CPA/Tax Preparer

Name: _____   **Phone:** _____

Property-Auto Insurance Agent

Name: _____   **Phone:** _____

Life Insurance Agent

Name: _____   **Phone:** _____

Other: _____

Name: _____   **Phone:** _____

Other: _____

Name: _____   **Phone:** _____

Other: _____

Name: _____   **Phone:** _____

Smart Retirement

LEGAL DOCUMENTS

Advance Directives   Location

Social Security Card: _____

Directives to Physicians: _____

Declaration for Mental Health: _____

Out of Hospital

Do Not Resuscitate: _____

Hospital Do Not Resuscitate: _____

Medical Power of Attorney: _____

HIPAA Power of Attorney: _____

Financial Power of Attorney: _____

Organ Donation Statement: _____

Other Legal Documents

Original Copy of Will: _____

Copies of Will: _____

Marriage License: _____

Pre-nuptial Agreement: _____

Trust Agreements: _____

Birth Certificate: _____

Adoption Papers: _____

Divorce Papers: _____

Citizenship/Naturalization

Papers: _____

Military Discharge/DD214: _____

Appendix 4

Smart Retirement

Asset Documents   **Location**

Home Deed: _____

Other Property Deed: _____

Other Property Deed: _____

Car Title: _____

Other Vehicle Title: _____

Other Documents: _____

_____

_____

_____

Credit Cards

Bank Name: _____

Credit Card Number: _____

Bank Name: _____

Credit Card Number: _____

Bank Name: _____

Credit Card Number: _____

Bank Name: _____

Credit Card Number: _____

_____

_____

_____

Smart Retirement

Banking Documents	**Location**
Bank Name:	_____
Checking Acct Num/Statement:	_____
Checking Acct Num/Statement:	_____
Checking Acct Num/Statement:	_____
Checking Acct Num/Statement:	_____
Sav Acct Num/Statement:	_____
Sav Acct Num/Statement:	_____
CD Num/Statement:	_____
CD Num/Statement:	_____
CD Num/Statement:	_____
CD Num/Statement:	_____
Bank Name:	_____
Checking Acct Num/Statement:	_____
Checking Acct Num/Statement:	_____
Checking Acct Num/Statement:	_____
Checking Acct Num/Statement:	_____
Sav Acct/Statement:	_____
Sav Acct/Statement:	_____
CD Num/Statement:	_____
CD Num/Statement:	_____
CD Num/Statement:	_____
CD Num/Statement:	_____

Appendix 4

Smart Retirement

Payable on Death All Accounts: _____

Mortgage

Bank/Acct Num: _____

Bank/Acct Num: _____

Investment Accounts   **Location**

Product/Statement: _____

_____

_____

_____

_____

_____

_____

_____

_____

_____

_____

_____

_____

_____

_____

_____

_____

_____

_____

_____

Smart Retirement

Transfer on Death or

Beneficiary: _____

Life Insurance   Location

Company: _____

Policy: _____

Company: _____

Policy: _____

Company: _____

Policy: _____

Health Insurance

Medicare Card: _____

Supplemental/Advantage Card: _____

Medicaid Card: _____

Other Ins Card: _____

FAS/HAS: _____

Property/Casualty Insurance

Auto Ins Co/Account: _____

Homeowners Co/Account: _____

Other Ins/Account: _____

Other Ins/Account: _____

Long Term Care

Company: _____

Policy: _____

Appendix 4

Smart Retirement

Burial Policy

Company: _____

Policy: _____

Tax Returns   **Location**

Last Two Years Returns: _____

Financial Plan _____

Smart Retirement

FUNERAL WISHES

Pre-Funeral Wishes

Organs Donated: Yes: ☐   No: ☐

All organs or selected   _____

Named Institution   _____

Funeral Wishes

Burial: ☐   Cremation: ☐

Funeral Service: Yes: ☐   No: ☐

If Funeral Service desired:

Open Casket or Closed: _____

Burial Clothing (ie: Military Uniform, etc.):   _____

Jewelry Items (worn or buried with me):   _____

Ashes in Urn: _____

If Veteran, Military honors: _____

Religious or Secular Service: _____

If Religious, which church: _____

Officiant (and one alternate):   _____

Specific Prayers/Verses/Poems: _____

Specific Music: _____

Specific People to Speak at Service: _____

Specific People for Pall Bearers: _____

_____

Do I want a Grave-side service: _____

Appendix 5

Smart Retirement

FUNERAL WISHES

Religious/Traditional Mourning Events: _____

Pre-Paid Funeral: _____

Funeral Home Preferences: _____

_____

Pre-Purchased Burial Plot: _____

Cemetery Preferences: _____

_____

Type of Headstone/Wording: _____

_____

Where should Obituary Run: _____

Factsheet for Obituary: _____

Specifics for Obituary: _____

_____

_____

Who should be notified of my death: _____

_____

_____

Charities in lieu of flowers: _____

If Cremated, disposition of ashes: _____

What should be done with my pets: _____

If no prepaid funeral package, where will
Funeral expense money come from: _____

Appendix 5

FUNERAL WISHES: OTHER NOTES

_____
_____
_____
_____
_____
_____
_____

> **Record Me Now app:**
> The following is a link for downloading a free app that will allow you to record and leave a personal video of messages for your family and loved ones. The app requires a webcam and includes the most important questions to address, based on the company's 5 years of research.
> **www.recordmenow.org**

Smart Retirement

FUNERAL PRICING COMPARISON WORKSHEET

Funeral Home 1: _____

Director's Name: _____

Phone Number: _____

Funeral Home 2: _____

Director's Name: _____

Phone Number: _____

Funeral Home 3: _____

Director's Name: _____

Phone Number: _____

	Funeral Home 1	Funeral Home 2	Funeral Home 3
Simple disposition of remains:			
Immediate Burial $	_____	_____	_____
Immediate Cremation: $	_____	_____	_____
Donation of Body $	_____	_____	_____
Donation of Body $	_____	_____	_____
Traditional Full Service:			
Basic Package $	_____	_____	_____

Basic Package includes: _____

_____

_____

Smart Retirement

		Funeral Home 1	Funeral Home 2	Funeral Home 3
Line Item Costs:				
Director and Staff	$	_____	_____	_____
Pick-Up of Body	$	_____	_____	_____
Embalming	$	_____	_____	_____
Storage	$	_____	_____	_____
Other Preparation	$	_____	_____	_____
Least Expensive Casket	$	_____	_____	_____
Name/Model #	$	_____	_____	_____
Outer Burial Container	$	_____	_____	_____
Viewing Cost per Day	$	_____	_____	_____
Memorial Service	$	_____	_____	_____
Hearse	$	_____	_____	_____
Other Vehicles	$	_____	_____	_____
Graveside Service	$	_____	_____	_____
Total Cost	$	_____	_____	_____
Cemetery Costs:				
Plot/Crypt	$	_____	_____	_____
Opening/Closing of Grave	$	_____	_____	_____
Perpetual Care	$	_____	_____	_____
Grave Liner	$	_____	_____	_____
Marker Monument	$	_____	_____	_____
Installing Marker/Monument	$	_____	_____	_____

Appendix 5

Smart Retirement

> **Additional Information on Funeral Pricing**
> **Federal Trade Commission**
> Source and for additional information:
>
> www.consumer.ftc.gov/articles/0301-funeral-costs-and-pricing-checklist

Smart Retirement

Spending Plan Template

Current Income and Expenses

	Weekly	Monthly	Annual
Income:			
Social Security Income	$_____	$_____	$_____
Pension	$_____	$_____	$_____
Annuity	$_____	$_____	$_____
Interest/Dividend Income	$_____	$_____	$_____
Rental Property Income	$_____	$_____	$_____
IRA Withdrawals	$_____	$_____	$_____
Other Savings	$_____	$_____	$_____
Other Income	$_____	$_____	$_____
Other Income	$_____	$_____	$_____
Other Income	$_____	$_____	$_____
Expected Inheritance Amount	$_____		
Expenses:			
Income Taxes (Prior Year)			$_____
Property Taxes			$_____
Mortgage or Rent	$_____	$_____	$_____
Food	$_____	$_____	$_____
Utilities	$_____	$_____	$_____
Electricity	$_____	$_____	$_____
Gas	$_____	$_____	$_____
Water	$_____	$_____	$_____

Smart Retirement

	Weekly	Monthly	Annual
Cable TV/Internet	$	$	$
Phone	$	$	$
Cell Phone	$	$	$
Home Insurance Premiums	$	$	$
Home Maintenance	$	$	$
Automobile Loan/Lease	$	$	$
Automobile Loan/Lease	$	$	$
Auto Insurance Premiums	$	$	$
Auto Maintenance	$	$	$
Medical/Co-Pay	$	$	$
Rx Medicines/Co-Pay	$	$	$
Dental/Co-Pay	$	$	$
Vision/Co-Pay	$	$	$
Medicare Premiums	$	$	$
Advantage/Supplemental Premiums	$	$	$
Other Health Ins Premiums	$	$	$
Long Term Care Premiums	$	$	$
Life Insurance Premiums	$	$	$
Clothing	$	$	$
Entertainment	$	$	$
Credit Card Interest	$	$	$
Other Loan Payments	$	$	$
Other Expenses _____	$	$	$

Smart Retirement

	Weekly	Monthly	Annual
Other Expenses_____	$_____	$_____	$_____
Other Expenses_____	$_____	$_____	$_____
Other Expenses_____	$_____	$_____	$_____
Other Expenses_____	$_____	$_____	$_____

Other Notes (including anticipated future increases, decreases, or additional items):

_____

_____

_____

_____

_____

_____

_____

_____

_____

_____

Smart Retirement

Investment Assets

Property and Real Estate Owned

Property 1:	Market Value	$_____
	Equity	$_____
Property 2:	Market Value	$_____
	Equity	$_____

Other Saleable Assets   Saleable Value

Asset: _____ $_____

Asset: _____ $_____

Asset: _____ $_____

Asset: _____ $_____

Asset: _____ $_____

Asset: _____ $_____

Texas Advance Directives Forms

The Texas Department of Aging and Disability Services provides a template of each of the Advance Directive forms mentioned in this text. Since the laws of Texas, or any state, are subject to change at any time, and to help keep this text up-to-date, a link to this website is provided below. Accessing the forms through the website should ensure that you are seeing the most current version of any of the forms:

https://hhs.texas.gov/laws-regulations/forms/advance-directives

As a final reminder, everyone's circumstances are different, and relying solely on a form downloaded from the internet could have unintended and potentially serious consequences. Therefore, as was repeated over and over again in this text, it is highly recommended that you seek the advice of a qualified Attorney to ensure that:
- All documents are properly drawn;
- All legal, tax, and financial consequences are fully understood; and
- All documents are in compliance with the laws of your state.

If you do not have an attorney, please refer to the Chapter on Hiring Professional Advisors earlier in this text.

Starting the End of Life Conversation
Questions to Help Get You Started

What matters most to me at the end of life?

_____

As a patient, I would like to know only the basics about my condition and treatment or do I want to know all of the details:

_____

If I am critically ill, I would allow my doctors the freedom doctors to do what they think is best, or do I want to have a say in every decision:

_____

If I have a terminal illness, would I prefer not to know how quickly it is progressing or to know my doctor's best estimation (ie: what role do I want to have in the decision-making process):

_____

If I have a terminal illness, would I want to receive medical care indefinitely, regardless of the side effects, or would I just want to be made comfortable:

_____

Do I want to spend my last days at home or in a health-care facility:

_____

How involved do I want my loved ones to be in my end of life decision making process: do I want them to follow my instructions exactly or do I want to do what brings them the most peace:

_____

As end of life nears, would I prefer to be alone be alone or surrounded by my loved ones?

_____

Smart Retirement

When it comes to sharing information, do I want my loved ones to know every detail, or only what I choose to tell them?

_____

What do you feel are the three most important things that you want your family, your friends, and/or your doctors to understand about your end-of-life wishes and preferences:

_____

_____

_____

Who do you want included in this end-of-life discussion:

_____

_____

_____

When would be the best time to have this discussion:

_____

Where would you be most comfortable having this discussion:

_____

What do you want to be sure to say:

_____

_____

_____

Questionnaire Courtesy of Houston Hospice
www.houstonhospice.org

Smart Retirement

Appendix 9

Life Expectancy Calculators

Using the Tools to Create an Individualized Estimate

As noted in above, the use of averages is useful in illustrating a broader point, yet individuals will probably want to create a customized estimate for themselves, based on their own particular health, family history, and longevity factors. The three tools that were presented and explained in the Healthcare Cost in Retirement chapter can be very useful in this regard, and the following worksheet and step-by-step instructions may be helpful in creating your own model; Note that you will need to have access to a computer and to the internet:

Step 1: Life Expectancy Calculator
Go to www.livingto100.com; answer the questions and obtain your personalized estimate of how old you will live to be; record this number for use in the following steps.

Step 2: Longevity Perspectives
Go to www.longevityillustrator.org; answer the questions and obtain the following graphs:
1. Graph showing a range of ages and the statistical probability that you will live to each of the various ages.
2. Planning Horizon Bar Graph showing the number of years you can expect to live with a given probability
3. Probability of living a specified number of years graph; Instead of showing the years you might expect to live with a specific level of certainty, this chart shows the probability that you will live a specific number of years in the future

While this step may not give you a definitive number like the first step does, it will give you an interesting perspective, using probability statistics, as to the various ages that you might live to; using these probabilities, you may want to consider refining the estimated age obtained in Step 1 of this exercise.

Step 3: Healthcare Cost Calculator
Go to www.aarp.org/retirement/the-aarp-healthcare-costs-calculator/; answer the questions; note that one of the questions you will be asked is "What age do you expect to live to?" You can use the estimated age obtained in the steps above to answer this question. The initial results presented will be:
- Your Total Estimated Healthcare Costs
- The estimated amount of these costs that will be covered by Medicare
- The estimated shortfall that you will have to pay out of pocket

Step 4: Impact of Certain Health Conditions
Under the graph of Healthcare Costs from the prior step is a button labeled "Health Conditions"; clicking this button will bring up another screen, and allow you to enter

any number of health conditions that you may have now, or anticipate that you might have based on your family history (hover cursor over "click to view entire list"; a comprehensive list of conditions will be displayed; the system will allow you to then click to select any combination of conditions). The updated results presented will be:

- Your Total Estimated Healthcare Costs
- The estimated amount of these costs that will be covered by Medicare
- The estimated shortfall that you will have to pay out of pocket

You are invited to experiment with selecting various combinations of health conditions, by again clicking on "click to view entire list"; you will be able to turn off and turn on various conditions merely by clicking the box next to the condition.

Step 5: Take Action
This is both a fascinating and an eye-opening exercise, and can give you a more personalized estimate of the Healthcare Costs that you will be faced with during your retirement years. It is highly recommended, then, that you share these results with your Financial Advisor and jointly create a plan for including these costs in your overall Retirement Financial Plan.

Medicare 2020 Summary of Costs

Source: www.medicare.gov/your-medicare-costs/costs-at-a-glance/costs-at-glance.html

Listed below are basic costs associated with Medicare. For specific cost information (like whether you've met your deductible, how much you'll pay for an item or service you received, or the status of a claim), visit: MyMedicare.gov.

2020 costs at a glance	
Part A premium	Most people don't pay a monthly premium for Part A (sometimes called "premium-free Part A"). If you buy Part A, you'll pay up to $458 each month in 2020. If you paid Medicare taxes for less than 30 quarters, the standard Part A premium is $458. If you paid Medicare taxes for 30-39 quarters, the standard Part A premium is $252.
Part A hospital inpatient deductible and coinsurance	You pay: • $1,408 deductible for each benefit period • Days 1-60: $0 coinsurance for each benefit period • Days 61-90: $352 coinsurance per day of each benefit period • Days 91 and beyond: $704 coinsurance per each "lifetime reserve day" after day 90 for each benefit period (up to 60 days over your lifetime) **Beyond lifetime reserve days: all costs**
Part B premium	The standard Part B premium amount is $144.60 (or higher depending on your income).
Part B deductible and coinsurance	$198. After your deductible is met, you typically pay 20% of the Medicare-approved amount for most doctor services (including most doctor services while you're a hospital inpatient), outpatient therapy, and Durable medical equipment (DME).
Part C premium	The Part C monthly premium varies by plan.

Appendix 10

Part D premium	The Part D monthly premium varies by plan (higher-income consumers may pay more).

Detailed Medicare cost information for 2020
Medicare Part A Hospital Insurance

- **Monthly premium**:
  Most people don't pay a monthly premium for Part A (sometimes called "premium-free Part A"). If you buy Part A, you'll pay up to $458. If you paid Medicare taxes for less than 30 quarters, the standard Part A premium is $458. If you paid Medicare taxes for 30-39 quarters, the standard Part A premium is $252.
- **Late enrollment penalty**:
  If you don't buy it when you're first eligible, your monthly premium may go up 10%. (You'll have to pay the higher premium for twice the number of years you could have had Part A, but didn't sign up.)

- Home health care
  - $0 for medically necessary home health care services.
  - 20% of the Medicare-approved amount for durable medical equipment.

- Hospice care
  - $0 for hospice care.
  - You may need to pay a copayment of no more than $5 for each prescription drug and other similar products for pain relief and symptom control while you're at home. In the rare case your drug isn't covered by the hospice benefit, your hospice provider should contact your Medicare drug plan to see if it's covered under Part D.
  - You may need to pay 5% of the Medicare-approved amount for inpatient respite care.
  - Medicare doesn't cover room and board when you get hospice care in your home or another facility where you live (like a nursing home)

- Hospital inpatient stay
  - $1,408 Deductible for each Benefit Period .
  - Days 1–60: $0 Coinsurance per day of each benefit period.
  - Days 61–90: $352 coinsurance per day of each benefit period.
  - Days 91 and beyond: $704 coinsurance per each "lifetime reserve day" after day 90 for each benefit period (up to 60 days over your lifetime).
  - Beyond Lifetime reserve days : all costs.
  - 20% of the Medicare-approved amount for mental health services you get from doctors and other providers while you're a hospital inpatient.

Note

You pay for private-duty nursing, a television, or a phone in your room. You pay for a private room unless it's medically necessary.

Mental health inpatient stay
- $1,408 Deductible for each Benefit Period .
- Days 1–60: $0 Coinsurance per day of each benefit period.
- Days 61–90: $352 coinsurance per day of each benefit period.
- Days 91 and beyond: $704 coinsurance per each "lifetime reserve day" after day 90 for each benefit period (up to 60 days over your lifetime).
- Beyond Lifetime reserve days : all costs.
- 20% of the Medicare-approved amount for mental health services you get from doctors and other providers while you're a hospital inpatient.

Note

There's no limit to the number of benefit periods you can have when you get mental health care in a general hospital. You can also have multiple benefit periods when you get care in a psychiatric hospital. Remember, there's a lifetime limit of 190 days.

- Skilled nursing facility stay
    - Days 1–20: $0 for each benefit period.
    - Days 21–100: $176 Coinsurance per day of each benefit period
    - Days 101 and beyond: all costs.

Medicare Part B (Medical Insurance)

- **Monthly premium:**

The standard Part B premium amount in 2020 will be $144.60. Most people will pay the standard Part B premium amount. If you modified adjusted gross income as reported on your IRS tax return from 2 years ago is above a certain amount, you'll pay the standard premium amount and an Income Related Monthly Adjustment Amount (IRMAA). IRMAA is an extra charge added to your premium.

Surcharge Table for Higher-Income Earners

If your yearly income in 2018 (for what you pay in 2020) was			You pay each month (in 2018)
File individual tax return	**File joint tax return**	**File married & separate tax return**	
$87,000 or less	$174,000 or less	$87,000 or less	$144.60

Appendix 10

above $87,000 up to $109,000	above $174,000 up to $218,000	Not applicable	$202.40
above $109,000 up to $136,000	above $218,000 up to $272,000	Not applicable	$289.20
above $136,000 up to $163,000	above $272,000 up to $326,000	Not applicable	$376.00
above $163,000 and less than $500,000	above $326,000 and less than $750,000	above $87,000 and less than $413,000	$462.70
$500,000 or above	$750,000 and above	$413,000 and above	$491.60

- **Late enrollment penalty:**

   In most cases, if you don't sign up for Part B when you're first eligible, you'll have to pay a late enrollment penalty. You'll have to pay this penalty for as long as you have Part B. Your monthly premium for Part B may go up 10% for each full 12-month period that you could have had Part B, but didn't sign up for it. Also, you may have to wait until the General Enrollment Period (from January 1 to March 31) to enroll in Part B. Coverage will start July 1 of that year.

- **Part B annual deductible:**
   You pay $198 per year for your Part B deductible. After your deductible is met, you typically pay 20% of the Medicare-approved amount for these:
    - Most doctor services (including most doctor services while you're a hospital inpatient)
    - Outpatient therapy
    - Durable medical equipment

- **Clinical laboratory services:**
   You pay $0 for Medicare-approved services.

- **Home health services:**
    - $0 for home health care services.
    - 20% of the Medicare-approved amount for durable medical equipment.

- **Medical and other services:**

Appendix 10

You pay 20% of the Medicare-approved amount for most doctor services (including most doctor services while you're a hospital inpatient), outpatient therapy, and durable medical equipment.

Note

Currently there may be limits on physical therapy, occupational therapy, and speech language pathology services. If so, there may be exceptions to these limits.

- **Outpatient mental health services:**
    - You pay nothing for your yearly depression screening if your doctor or health care provider accepts assignment.
    - 20% of the Medicare-approved amount for visits to your doctor or other health care provider to diagnose or treat your condition. The Part B deductible applies.
    - If you get your services in a hospital outpatient clinic or hospital outpatient department, you may have to pay an additional copayment or coinsurance amount to the hospital.

- **Partial hospitalization mental health services:**
You pay a percentage of the Medicare-approved amount for each service you get from a doctor or certain other qualified mental health professionals if your health care professional accepts assignment. You also pay coinsurance for each day of partial hospitalization services provided in a hospital outpatient setting or community mental health center, and the Part B deductible applies.

- **Outpatient hospital services:**
    - You generally pay 20% of the Medicare-approved amount for the doctor or other health care provider's services, and the Part B deductible applies.
    - For all other services, you also generally pay a copayment for each service you get in an outpatient hospital setting. You may pay more for services you get in a hospital outpatient setting than you would pay for the same care in a doctor's office.
    - For some screenings and preventive services, coinsurance, copayments, and the Part B deductible don't apply (so you pay nothing).

Medicare Part C (Medicare Advantage)

Medicare Part C is known as Medicare Advantage. These are private plans run by private insurance companies that, by law, must at least be "equivalent" to regular Medicare **Part A** and **Part B** coverage, yet there are tremendous variations on the various options the plans offer; some offer prescription drug coverage, for example, and some do not. The monthly premium varies widely depending on your state and the private insurer you choose, as well as whether you choose an HMO or PPO for your Medicare Advantage coverage. Medicare Advantage Plans are further described in an earlier Chapter entitled "**Understanding Medicare**"

One other important note: if you have a Medicare Advantage plan, any **Medigap** policy (Medicare Supplement Policy) would be useless, as a Medigap plan will not pay if you are covered by a Medicare Advantage Plan.

Medicare Part D (Medicare prescription drug coverage)

- **Monthly premium:**

The Part D monthly premium varies by plan (higher-income consumers may pay more). The chart below shows your estimated prescription drug plan monthly premium based on your income as reported on your IRS tax return. If your income is above a certain limit, you'll pay an income-related monthly adjustment amount in addition to your plan premium.

Surcharge Table for Higher-Income Earners

If your filing status and yearly income in 2018 was			
File individual tax return	File joint tax return	File married & separate tax return	You pay each month (in 2018)
above $109,000 up to $136,000	above $218,000 up to $272,000	Not applicable	$289.20
above $136,000 up to $163,000	above $272,000 up to $326,000	Not applicable	$376.00
above $163,000 and less than $500,000	above $326,000 and less than $750,000	above $87,000 and less than $413,000	$462.70
$500,000 or above	$750,000 and above	$413,000 and above	$491.60
above $109,000 up to $136,000	above $218,000 up to $272,000	Not applicable	$289.20

Appendix 10

| $500,000 or above | $750,000 and above | $413,000 and above | $76.40 + your plan premium |

- **Late enrollment penalty:**

You may owe a late enrollment penalty if, for any continuous period of 63 days or more after your Initial Enrollment Period is over, you go without one of these:
- A Medicare Prescription Drug Plan (Part D)
- A Medicare Advantage Plan (Part C) (like an HMO or PPO)
- Another Medicare health plan that offers Medicare prescription drug coverage
- Creditable prescription drug coverage
- In general, you'll have to pay this penalty for as long as you have a Medicare drug plan. The cost of the late enrollment penalty depends on how long you went without Part D or creditable prescription drug coverage. Learn more about the Part D late enrollment penalty.

- **Deductibles, copayments, & coinsurance:**

The amount you pay for Part D deductibles, copayments, and/or coinsurance varies by plan. For more specific information, visit **https://www.medicare.gov/find-a-plan/questions/home.aspx**, and then call the plans you're interested in to get more details.

SOCIAL SECURITY RETIREMENT AGE INFORMATION

Social Security Full Retirement Age Chart

Year of Birth *	Full Retirement Age
1937 or earlier	65
1938	65 and 2 months
1939	65 and 4 months
1940	65 and 6 months
1941	65 and 8 months
1942	65 and 10 months
1943 - 1954	66
1955	66 and 2 months
1956	66 and 4 months
1957	66 and 6 months
1958	66 and 8 months
1959	66 and 10 months
1960 and later	67

*If you were born on January 1st of any year you should refer to the previous year. (If you were born on the 1st of the month, we figure your benefit (and your full retirement age) as if your birthday was in the previous month.)

Smart Retirement

What if you apply for benefits early?
If you apply for Social Security Benefits before your Full Retirement Age (FRA), you will received a reduction in benefits according to the following table:

Apply at age	If FRA = 66	If FRA = 67
62	75.0%	70%
63	80.0%	75%
64	86.7%	80%
65	93.3%	86.7%
66	100%	93.3%
67		100%

Note: The earliest you can start receiving Social Security retirement benefits remains age 62.

What if you apply for benefits after Full Retirement Age?
If you apply for Social Security Benefits after your Full Retirement Age (FRA), you will earn an 8% increase in delayed credits, according to the following table:

Apply at age	Benefit will be % if FRA = 66	Benefit will be % if FRA = 67
66	100%	93.3%
67	108%	100%
68	116%	108%
69	124%	116%
70	132%	124%

Note: The delayed credits stop at age 70; delaying taking Social Security Retirement benefits after age 70 will not result in any further 8% annual increases.

Smart Retirement

Appendix 12

Smart Retirement

Retirement Life Plan

Throughout our pre-retirement years, our time, our focus, and our goals centered on and around family, raising children, and work; often we have been so overwhelmed that we never took the time to formally understand what truly makes us happy and to formulate our life's goals. As we enter our retirement years, however, we now have an opportunity to take control of our future direction, to understand what motivates us and leaves us with an ongoing sense fulfillment and contentment. It even allows us to reinvent ourselves on many different levels. You are encouraged to take this exercise seriously, as it could be the foundation for a happy and fulfilling life in retirement. Sit and ponder this alone, and share your thoughts and ideas with your spouse, partner, or closest friend.

The exercise has multiple parts:
1. Life Satisfaction Survey
2. Vision Statement for Retirement
3. Understanding and Defining what makes us happy
4. Understanding and Defining our Personal Values
5. Defining Our Initial Goals for Retirement
6. Creating our Retirement Life Plan

Each page has a brief explanation and some examples to get you started. Good luck, and have a great retirement.

How Satisfied Are You?

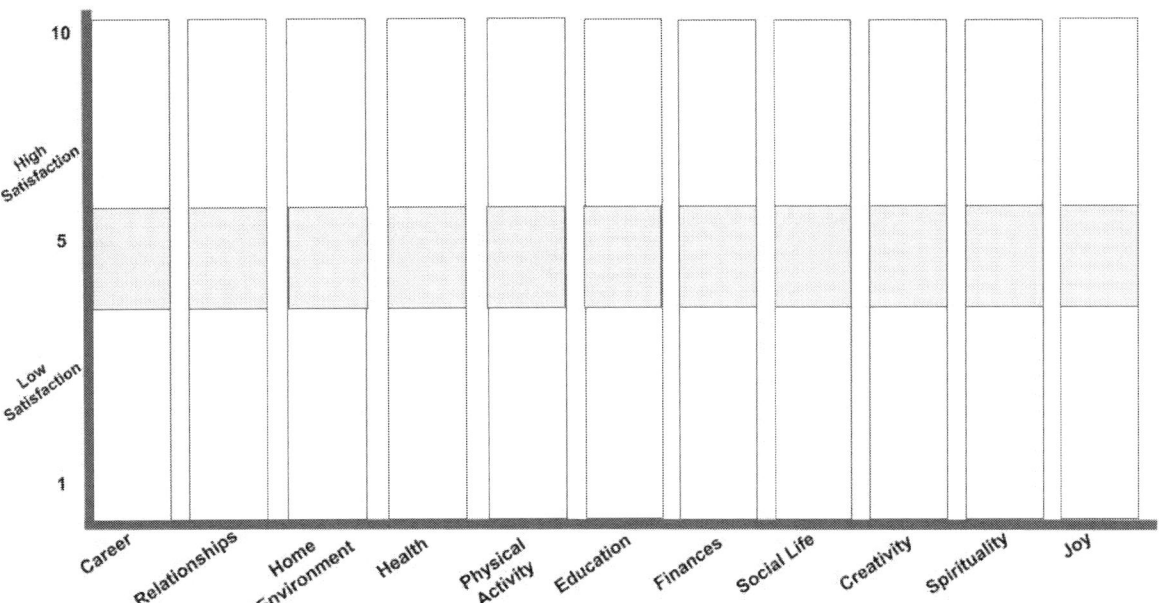

Appendix 12

Smart Retirement

What Are You Going to Do?
Thinking about each of the categories above that you scored less than High Satisfactions, think of two or three things that you might be able to do to bring the score up into the High Satisfaction range.

Career: _____

_____

_____

Relationships: _____

_____

_____

Home: _____

_____

_____

Health: _____

_____

_____

Physical: _____

_____

Education: _____

_____

_____

Smart Retirement

Finances: _____

_____

_____

Social: _____

_____

_____

Creativity: _____

_____

_____

Spiritual: _____

_____

_____

Joy: _____

_____

_____

Smart Retirement

Your Vision Statement

A Vision Statement is a high-level declaration of your objectives and intentions; it is a picture of what you want your future to look like, the framework and inspiration for your life in retirement. Don't confuse the Vision Statement with a roadmap; it is not tied to the details, but it should be the compass for setting the direction for your life in retirement. Examples of Vision Statement components would be: learn one or more new hobbies; work part-time doing something that I love; take more vacations; move to a warmer climate or a new location on a beach. These are declarations of your dreams, what you would like your retirement life to be, even if something doesn't seem possible at the moment (remember, in the early 1960s no one thought it would be possible to put a man on the moon until then President Kennedy gave us that challenge).

The Vision Statement, then, is high-level and conceptual; you can use the space below for documenting your Vision Statement:

_____

_____

_____

_____

_____

_____

_____

_____

_____

_____

Understanding What Makes Me Happy

The following list was created as a starting point for discovering your very own deep-seated needs and desires. Circle the ones that resonate with you, then add your own at the bottom of the page.

Being with friends
Being married or having a special partner
Taking care of others
Having a close family
Having good friends
Making a contribution to the world
Participating in sports or hobbies
Having financial security
Being healthy and physically fit
Learning new things
Staying busy/ being productive
Making money
Having a purpose
Volunteering
Helping others
Being emotionally stable
Being independent
Not being a burden on family
Living in my own home
Spending time with grandkids

Continue your own list below:

_____

_____

_____

_____

_____

_____

_____

Smart Retirement

Values

Values are a person's underlying principles or standards that drive our behavior; they have no start and end like a goal, they are ongoing, never ceasing. It has been said that Goals give us a reason to wake up in the morning, and Values help us sleep at night. Circle the ones that you want to live by, then add your own at the bottom of the page.

Compassion	Faith	Responsibility
Spirituality	Love	Courtesy
Passion	Genuineness	Honesty
Forgiveness	Self Esteem	Transparency
Flexibility	Rationality	Integrity
Self-Acceptance	Faithfulness	Loyalty
Dependability	Caring	Open-Mindedness
Openness	Humility	Consistency
Cooperation	Self-Control	
Hope	Commitment	

Continue your own list below:

_____

_____

_____

_____

_____

_____

_____

_____

Smart Retirement

Goals:

The dictionary defines goal as the end result of a person's effort or aim; the object of what a person is striving for; a measurable outcome. It could be a broad, lifestyle change such as attaining a degree, learning a language, quitting smoking and becoming physically fit and healthy. It might also be the attainment of a dream, travel to a specific destination, or purchasing that lakefront property. Retirement represents a rare opportunity to define, redefine, reestablish or create new goals for yourself, yet there is nothing cast in concrete. If you start down a path and find you don't really like the direction, change it, and if you achieve a goal, replace it with another. Using the results of the prior exercise (Understanding and defining What Makes You Happy), create a list of your own goals that you will carry into retirement.

_____

_____

_____

_____

_____

_____

_____

_____

_____

_____

_____

_____

_____

Smart Retirement

Retirement Life Plan

The Retirement Life Plan is a refinement of the above exercises, where we:
- Re-examine each of selections that we made in each of the above sections
- Identify the 5 most important Things that Make us Happy, the 5 most important Values, and the 3 most important Short Term, Medium Term, and Long Term Goals
- Document our Retirement Life Plan in the section below

Top Five Things that Make Us Happy

_____

_____

_____

_____

_____

Top Five Values

_____

_____

_____

_____

_____

Appendix 12

Smart Retirement

Top 3 Short Term Goals

_____

_____

_____

Top 3 Medium Term Goals

_____

_____

_____

Top 3 Long Term Goals

_____

_____

_____

Notes:

_____

_____

_____

_____

Made in the USA
Monee, IL
12 October 2020